Contents

François Le Berre

THE NEW CHAMELEON HANDBOOK

Everything About Selection, Care,
Diet, Disease, Reproduction, and Behavior

with 108 Color Photographs

BARRON'S

Dedication

I dedicate this book to André Peyrieras, whose knowledge is equalled only by his generosity. May he find herein the proof of my profound gratitude.

All inquiries should be addressed to:
Barron's Educational Series, Inc.
250 Wireless Boulevard
Hauppauge, New York 11788

International Standard Book No. 0-8120-1805-2

Library of Congress Catalog Card No. 94-48911

Library of Congress Cataloging-in-Publication Data

LeBerre, François.
  The new chameleon handbook : everything about selection, care, diet, disease, reproduction, and behavior / François LeBerre.
      p.   cm.
    Includes index.
    ISBN 0-8120-1805-2
    1. Chameleons as pets. 2. Chameleons.
    I. Title.
SF459.C45L425   1995
639.3′95—dc20   94-48911
                                                CIP

Printed in Hong Kong

56789   9955   987654321

(M)639.395 B

About the Author

François LeBerre was born in Montreal and grew up in Africa. As a child he was drawn to chameleons by their gentle demeanor and expressive gaze. This early fascination led to a lifelong pursuit. With André Peyrieras, the eminent Malagasy naturalist, he has developed a chameleon breeding program in Madagascar. M. LeBerre continues to search the forests, looking for rare species and trying to better understand chameleon behavior.

Photo Credits

Wolfgang Schmidt: pages 12, 74, 75, 96, 107 (top); John Uhern: page 51; All other photographs were taken by the author.

Photos on the Covers

Front: *Chamaeleo lateralis* (female)
Inside front: *Chamaeleo chameleon* (male)
Inside back: *Chamaeleo fischeri tavetanus* (female)
Back left: *Chamaeleo lateralis* (male)
Back left: *Chamaeleo minor* (female)

Important Note

Before using any of the electrical equipment described in this book, be sure to read Avoiding Electrical Accidents on page 54.

While handling chameleons you may occasionally receive bites or scratches. If your skin is broken, see your physician immediately.

Some terrarium plants may be harmful to the skin or mucous membranes of human beings. If you notice any signs of irritation, wash the area thoroughly. See your physician if the condition persists.

Chameleons may transmit certain infections to humans. Always wash your hands carefully after handling your specimens. Always supervise children who wish to observe your chameleons.

Preface

"Their legs are fairly high; their back, scaly up to the end of the tail; they appear to be wearing a helmet; the skin on the flanks and the abdomen is flaccid and soft. This animal is very fearful and, when caught, walks very slowly. Some say it lives on the wind, which we witnessed to be false: it climbs trees and plants where it eats flies and other small insects, which it snatches quickly with its dart-like tongue.

"They are extremely shy and change color when something comes close to them. They can do this because of the thinness and transparency of their skin. When one finds them on the grass, they are perfectly green; when they become aware of the presence of others, they become white and black. Their eyes are quite small. The pupil, which is no larger than the head of a pin, sits in the middle of a fat little ball like a pea. They are always moving. Never do they close their eyes."

This is how François Martin de Vitre described the chameleons he encountered in Madagascar during his voyage to the Indies in 1602. A modern-day observer of these reptiles would doubtless find these notes as amusing as the creatures they describe, although the observations capture the chameleon's affected mannerisms quite accurately.

But, almost four centuries later, how much more can we claim to know about these fascinating creatures?

Chamaeleo quadricornis (male).

PART ONE
Biology and Ecology

More than 100 species of chameleons have been described. Many display surprisingly beautiful colors—which can change in ways that seem astonishing. Some have horns, crests, or other appendages that spark our curiosity. Their unusual appearance easily arouses the attention and even the affection of reptile enthusiasts.

However, in spite of this animal's famous morphological characteristics, most people know comparatively little about its habits. And, although chameleons are now readily available in the pet trade, useful literature regarding their needs in captivity is scarce.

The breeding of chameleons, whether for professional purposes or for pleasure, requires a certain amount of practical knowledge and a kind of empathy between the keeper and the kept. Even when they are cared for in spacious, naturalistic settings and offered climatic conditions approaching those of their natural habitats, these lizards can be difficult to keep and breed. It is always the keeper's responsibility to research the needs of the chameleons he or she keeps, then to provide the best possible environment for them. For example, some species will live happily in a terrarium, while others may need larger, more complex enclosures.

Much progress is being made in the field of reptile husbandry. Long dependent on collected wild specimens, the pet industry is now supplied with at least some captive-raised chameleons. The future efforts of enthusiastic reptile breeders will help preserve wild populations as well as increase the availability of healthy, farm-raised chameleons.

Quite apart from the interest I take in ecosystems and the reproduction of chameleons in terrariums, I feel a particular affinity to them. To my mind, only the good and the beautiful make life bearable. I believe chameleons possess both these qualities.

Chamaeleo willsii (female).

Chapter 1

What Are Chameleons?

The Different Genera of Chameleons

The family Chamaeleonidae, which contains all chameleons, consists of two subfamilies. The "typical" and the dwarf chameleons belong to the subfamily Chamaeleoninae; the "atypical" stump-tailed chameleons are members of the subfamily Brookesinae. Each of these groups is divided into two genera, each with its own characteristics. The genera in the Chamaeleoninae subfamily are *Chamaeleo*, established by Laurenti in 1768, and *Bradypodion*, defined by Fitzinger in 1843. The Brookesinae subfamily contains the genus *Brookesia*, established by Gray in 1865, and *Rhampholeon*, added by Günther in 1874.

Typical and Dwarf Chameleons—Subfamily Chamaeleoninae

The members of this subfamily are more agile, more capable of changing color, and equipped with a smoother skin and a proportion-ally longer, more prehensile tail than their stump-tailed cousins. The Chamaeleoninae range from slightly more than 2 inches (5 cm) to just under 3 feet (91 cm) in length.

- *Bradypodion* (from Greek *bradus podos*, "slow foot") are dwarf chameleons. This genus also has a single claw on each toe and a prehensile tail. In addition, it has wide parietal bones, which make its head appear broad. All the species in this genus have simple, single-lobed lungs and are ovoviviparous.
- *Chamaeleo* (from Greek *chamaileon*, "lion on the ground") are "typical" chameleons. This genus has a single claw on each toe, a prehensile tail, and—with the exception of *C. oustaleti*, which has pulmonary air sacs—bilobed lungs. There are both oviparous and ovoviviparous species.

Stump-tailed Chameleons—Subfamily Brookesinae

The stump-tailed chameleons are characterized by their slow movements and their failure to respond aggressively when seized. Besides these differences, they

Bradypodion thamnobates (male) in a threatening posture.

Chamaeleo pardalis (male).

have weakly prehensile or non-prehensile tails, and most have a complex scalation that features dorsolateral projections, spinous body scales, and supraorbital projections. They are small, ranging from slightly more than 1 to 4 inches (2.5–10.2 cm) in length.

• *Brookesia* (named in honor of the British naturalist Brookes) have single claws on each toe, a weakly prehensile tail, and simple lungs. All are oviparous.

• *Rhampholeon* (from Greek *rhamphos* + *leon*, "crawling lion"). The members of this genus have bifid claws on each toe. The tail is only weakly prehensile. These species have simple lungs and all are oviparous. Some taxonomists consider this genus in synonymy with Brookesia.

Although it may seem complicated, when discussing either member of the subfamily Chamaeleoninae in general, the term "chameleon" is

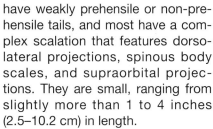
Brookesia thieli, found only in primary forests.

Rhampholeon kerstenii, found at the edges of secondary forests.

usually used. In technical discussions that pertain to both subfamilies, I will use the term "chameleonid." If additional clarification is necessary, I will refer to the members of the genus *Chamaeleo* as "typical chameleons," reserving "dwarf chameleons" for the members of the genus *Bradypodion*. "Stump-tailed chameleons" refers to all members of the subfamily Brookesinae—*Brookesia* and *Rampholeon* alike.

Morphology

As with all lizards, the body of the chameleonids is covered with scales. Although laterally flattened, when seen in profile chameleonids have a typical lacertiform (lizard-like) shape. The head is distinct from the neck, and the toes, tong-like in arrangement, are designed for tenacious grasping. Some species are strong, agile climbers; others favor terrestrial situations. Those species that have a strongly prehensile tail often have conical pads near the tail for extra grip. The inner surfaces of the feet are similarly equipped. The strong jaws contain rows of tiny, identical teeth.

Gender Identification

Most chameleonids show sexual differences (sexual dimorphism). Often, the males have secondary characteristics such as horns (*C. fülleborni*) or vertebral and/or caudal crests (*C. montium*) and are larger than the females. Gender-related color differences (sexual dichromatism) may also occur in some species (e.g., *C. cristatus*). In species that do not exhibit overt sexual differences, gender can often be determined by examining the base of the tail immediately behind the cloaca. If the specimen is a male, bilateral swellings caused by the hemipenes (copulatory organs) may often be seen.

Classification

Taxonomy, the science of classifying organisms, involves consideration of biological and morphological characteristics. This process, initially generalized, quickly becomes very detailed. Following a taxonomic classification is rather simple, however, and very enlightening. The method and terminology used for scientific identification are exemplified by the spectacular Mt. Kenyan Jackson's chameleon (See Table: Taxonomy of *Chamaeleo jacksonii xantholophus*).

Taxonomic position of chameleons

As the table shows, the taxonomic position of the Mt. Kenyan Jackson's chameleon is precise, and its identification is easy for researchers throughout the world. And what are some of the characteristics that make such exact classification possible? The fact that the creature is animate makes it an animal. Its backbone makes it a

Chamaeleo montium montium males have very little in common morphologically with their females. This specimen shows by his superb coloring that he is master of his territory.

Taxonomy of *Chamaeleo jacksonii xantholophus*

Kingdom: Animalia	Animal
Phylum: Chordata	Vertebrate, an animal with a backbone
Class: Reptilia	Reptile, the group containing chelonians (turtles, tortoises), crocodilians (alligators, crocodiles), rhynchocephalians (tuataras), and squamata
Order: Squamata	The group containing snakes, amphisbaenids, and lizards
Suborder: Lacertilia	Lizard
Family: Chamaeleonidae	Chameleonid
Subfamily: Chameleoninae	Typical and dwarf chameleons
Genus: *Chamaeleo*	Typical chameleon
Species: *jacksonii*	Jackson's chameleon
Subspecies: *xantholophus*	Giant Mt. Kenyan race

vertebrate. Its dry scaly skin and the fact that it is poikilothermic (cold-blooded) identify it as a reptile. Like most lizards, it has legs; the prehensile tail, syndactyloas (bundled) toes, turreted eyes, and laterally flattened body further tell us it is a chameleonid.

Let us examine the taxonomy of chameleonids in greater detail.

Genera, Species, and Subspecies and a Comment on Variation

The classification of chameleonids and the scientific names that have been given them (and all other animals and plants) are the results of careful consideration by taxonomists. Since each taxonomist/ researcher places special emphasis on his or her particular discipline, taxonomic decisions may differ somewhat. With time and further research, greater uniformity is likely.[3]

A *genus* is a grouping of related species with similar characteristics. As mentioned previously, I favor four genera of chameleons. Other people may recognize fewer or more.

The term *species* designates a group of creatures exhibiting the same characteristics, living in the same habitat, and able to breed

Chamaeleo parsonii cristifer (male).

among themselves. Species may be divided into subspecies.

A *subspecies* is a population geographically isolated from others in the species and presenting specific genetic characteristics different from the species type. Successful breedings between subspecies are possible.

Genera, Species and Subspecies of Chameleonids

Genus	Species	Subspecies
Chamaeleo	78[1]	50
Bradypodion	6[2]	4
Brookesia	23	1
Rhampholeon	7	4

Although a very few researchers recognize "variation" among chameleonids, such description is not widely accepted. A case in point is the designation of "variety" occasionally applied by some researchers to a form of *C. parsonii* that occurs near Perinet (Andasibe), Madagascar. Most modern researchers classify this as a subspecies, *C. parsonii cristifer.*

[1] One new chameleon from Mt. Marsabit, Kenya, has been described: *Chamaeleo marsabitensis,* Tilbury, 1991, increasing to 78 the number of species of Chamaeleo known today. A new species of *Brookesia, B. valeriae,* Raxworthy, 1992, increases the number of species in that genus to 23.

[2] Several researchers are currently working on the exact classifications of the species within the genus *Bradypodion.* New species may be described.

[3] Several authors have worked on the taxonomy of chameleons, and none of them agree on the way to group the species. While D. Hillenius, a Dutch scientist, worked on the morphological characteristics, W. Böhme and C. Kläver, both German scientists, focused on the structure of the hemipenes (a useful method when classifying snakes) and lungs to reorganize the nomenclature. But chameleons are not like snakes, and it is far easier to imagine relative groups by observing the babies of the different species. The young of all bear characteristic morphological features. For example, the babies of the very similar *C. parsonii* and *C. globifer* can be differentiated by careful observation. Those of *C. globifer* have white rings on their toes. These rings are lacking in the young of *C. parsonii.*

(top)
Chamaeleo parsonii juvenile.

(left)
Chamaeleo globifer juvenile.

Chapter 2
Characteristics of the Chameleonids' Range

Geographic Range

Chameleonids are distributed over a very large area, which includes much of Africa (excluding the central Saharan region), Madagascar, the islands in the Indian Ocean, a part of the Arabian Peninsula, Sri Lanka, India, and a small part of southern Europe.

The Geographic Range of Chameleonids (shown in purple).

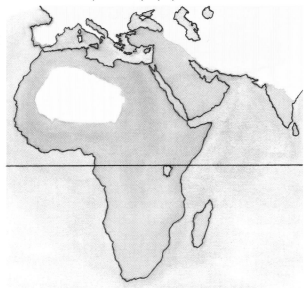

The vast majority of chameleonids live in forests or on the edges of areas with abundant vegetation. A few live in deserts, however. One such is the Namibian *Chamaeleo namaquensis*. Having no trees to protect it from the heat, this specialized chameleon may dig a burrow in which to take refuge. Although many typical and dwarf chameleons can be found in both primary (virgin) and secondary (regrown) forests, most stump-tailed chameleons are restricted to primary forests. They are usually absent from all other areas.

Tropical and Equatorial Climates

It is difficult to visualize the environmental needs of chameleons without knowing something about climatic effects. Both tropical and equatorial climates are quite variable. Such factors as sea and air currents, presence or lack of water sources, elevation, degree of forestation, and even soil quality can affect the climate.

Solar Energy and Radiance

Above the earth's atmosphere the sun emits approximately 1400 watts per square meter (8 percent ultraviolet, 51 percent infrared, and 41 percent visible light). While the sunlight traverses our atmosphere, this intensity is diminished considerably. At the surface of the earth the intensity has been reduced by about 30 percent, to approximately 1000 watts per square meter. The stated percentages of the spectrum change only slightly, measuring about 3 percent ultraviolet, 55 percent infrared, and 42 percent visible light on the ground.

Temperatures

Globally, the differences between 6:00 A.M. and noontime temperatures may vary considerably. Among other factors, latitude, altitude, time of year, and forest cover figure prominently.

At sea level in the equatorial zone, the difference is quite small. There, however, increasing altitude has the same effect as a change in latitude. Temperatures become cooler by 1.8°F (1°C) for each 600 feet (180 m) increase in elevation.

The average annual temperature for the southern hemisphere's Tropic of Capricorn is about 70°F (21°C). The northern hemisphere's Tropic of Cancer is a few degrees warmer, averaging 74°F (23.3°C).

Barometric Pressure

Although it is not yet certain, it is possible that changes in barometric readings, such as the falling pres-

Chamaeleo namaquensis, a Namibian species.

sure that accompanies storms, may have a considerable effect on chameleonid behavior. The barometric pressure in the tropics, a cyclonic zone, varies between 2.5 and 4 millibars. Normal day and night barometric pressures do not vary greatly. Additional studies need to be made.

Wind

Wind is created by differences in barometric pressure. Chameleonids are more active on windy days than on calm ones. Then, among the waving leaves and branches, they are difficult to detect. They move along the branches with more speed at these times.

Relative Humidity

The relative humidity of the atmosphere is expressed in percentages (hydrometric degrees). The average humidity of a desert zone is 25 percent; that of a savanna, 50 percent; and it is 90 percent in a forested equatorial region. Relative humidity reaches 100 percent (saturation) within a cloud or a tropical rainforest.

Morondavia Madagascar, a typical Sudano-Guinean region.

desert and mountain regions. The relative humidity in the atmosphere rises, and tiny droplets of water are deposited on cool surfaces. This permits both plants and animals to obtain water in otherwise arid zones.

Evaporation and lower relative humidity occur as a result of wind action and the sun's heat.

Rainfall

Tropical regions have two rainy seasons: one long and one short. Dry seasons intervene, their duration increasing as the distance from the equator increases. Maximum rainfall occurs when the sun is close to the equator (approaching or leaving equinox); periods of dryness occur when the sun is more distant (approaching or leaving solstice).

Atmospheric humidity varies considerably in the tropical regions of the world, but rather slightly at the equator itself.

Under favorable conditions a nighttime drop in temperature can lead to the formation of dew, a fairly regular occurrence in both

A forest in northeastern Madagascar.

Chapter 3
Elements of Chameleonid Ecology

Geographic Range by Genus

Members of the genus *Chamaeleo* are found throughout the range of the family Chamaeleonidae, but the other genera are much more restricted. *Rhampholeon* are found from equatorial Africa southward to South Africa, skirting the East African coast; *Bradypodion* are even more limited, occurring only in South Africa. *Brookesia* are not found outside Madagascar.

Most individual chameleonid species occupy rather narrow geographic ranges, with *Chamaeleo senegalensis, C. gracilis, C. chameleon*, and *Rhampholeon spectrum* being notable exceptions.

Habitats
The habitats occupied by chameleonids are very diverse. Common sites include grasslands, mountainous rain forests, or savannas. However, each species prefers a particular type of habitat: forested, wooded, grassy, shrubby, and so forth.

Chamaeleo and *Bradypodion* can be found in most types of vegetation, including xeric (arid) areas and secondary (degraded) forests. The stump-tailed chameleons, in contrast, are far less tolerant of their surroundings and require primary or untouched forest. Some species are so dependent on their specific habitat niche that if it disappeared, they would vanish with it. Others take advantage of the degradation of their habitat.

Chamaeleo jacksonii jacksonii juvenile basking in its Kenyan habitat.

Bradypodion (male). This is one of several undescribed chameleonids that can be found in Africa and Madagascar.

The stump-tailed chameleons require certain kinds of sites for egg deposition. Specifically, female stump-tails lay their eggs in piles of dead foliage on the forest floor, where the natural decomposition of the leaves provides a constant level of heat and humidity. If the forests are destroyed, the nesting places of the stump-tailed chameleons will vanish. Ultimately the chameleons themselves will perish.

Forest destruction obviously is a greater threat to the various species of *Brookesia* and *Rhampholeon* than to the other genera of chameleonids, which dig holes to lay their eggs. On the other hand, the small size of the stump-tails enables them to survive on a diet that would be entirely inadequate for larger chameleons. Primary in the diet of the stump-tails are insects such as small flies and termites. Such insects, along with tiny

beetles, mantids, and true bugs, are abundant in primary forests. Larger species of chameleons prefer grasshoppers, crickets, flies, caterpillars, spiders, snails, and other small animals as dietary staples. These larger prey are plentiful on the edges of degraded forests, but are not easily found in the forests themselves. Thus, the interior of a primary forest offers a much less attractive menu than do clearings, forest edges, or degraded forests.

Suppose we stick colored pins into a large map of Africa and Madagascar, each pin to represent a zone with a dense chamaeleonid population. Now superimpose another map showing climatic regions. The conclusion is obvious: the highest concentrations of chameleonids and the very localized species are found in the most humid areas or in those with the highest rainfall. E.-R. Brygoo[1] points out that the eastern region of Madagascar, mainly covered with deciduous forest or tropical rain forest, is very humid and has more than 50 percent of the living forms of chameleons—18 of the 35.

Environment and Species

Why are certain species found in one place and not another? Why can a particular genus live here but not there? As they evolved, the chameleonids became inextricably linked to their habitat. Over the years, each species adapted to a specific environment. When climatic changes altered that environment, the chameleonids were forced either to migrate in search of another, more favorable, habitat or to adapt. If they could neither migrate nor adapt, they died.

Thus, as the climate became untenably warm or cool on the plains or mountains of Africa and Madagascar, the chameleonid species found there adapted or dispersed. Those that dispersed colonized other, more hospitable, areas and diversified, first to subspecies, ultimately to full species. Inhospitable, uninhabitable areas separated and isolated populations, and the various populations became ever more distinct. The first changes in a population were subtle, perhaps a slight color change or shift in prey preference. As isolation continued, the changes became more pronounced, affecting adult size or cranial crests. Soon (in geologic terms) the existing populations developed the set of characteristics necessary for their survival, now looking very different from the original parent species. And another subspecies or species came into existence.

Camouflage: A Way of Life

Many people believe that the chameleonid changes color to resemble its surroundings. Indeed, some think that the surface on which it sits dictates the lizard's color.

Although it is true that the better a chameleon blends into its surroundings, the less likely it is to be eaten by a predator such as a snake or a bird, it is not the background that governs the lizard's color.

The methods of camouflage used by a chameleonid involve its body form and its manner of movement as well as its color. Its faltering gait resembles the movement of a wind-blown leaf. Its vertically flattened body enhances that illusion. Shifts of pattern also occur, and although a green lizard against a green background or a brown lizard against a brown background is more fully camouflaged, a brilliantly patterned displaying male is easily overlooked by a human observer.

The actual coloration of the chameleonid, which varies both by species and by gender, is less affected by the lizard's immediate surroundings than by a complex combination of external and internal cues. Among the former are light intensity and temperature, and among the latter are the emotional state and physical health of the lizard. The emotional state of the lizard is affected by many things, not the least important of which is the presence of other chameleonids (male or female) of the same species. (See page 22.)

Camouflage is very important for a creature that does not move quickly, yet is a predator. "Seeing without being seen" is a special and important adaptation. The stump-tailed chameleons of the subfamily

Brookesia vadoni (male). This species was found by André Peyrieras in 1968.

flaged, both by color and by body form. It is likely that researchers who consider these animals uncommon have stepped on or over many of them while walking in the forest!

The coloration of *Brookesia vadoni* has evolved to mimic the mossy environment in which the lizard lives. The cryptic outline and coloration of another species, *B. peyrierasi*, make the lizard appear much like a chip of wood when it plays dead. The high humidity in the habitat of *Rhampholeon spectrum* actually allows moss to grow on the skin of the lizard. This imparts to the chameleon the appearance of a dead leaf.

Young chameleonids have many predators, but the threat lessens as the animals mature. The lizards must employ convincing camouflage and mature quickly to reduce the risk of being eaten. It is interesting that the young of one species, *Chamaeleo oustaleti*, which lives in an arid climate where the trees have few leaves, have a very slender body form and a dull red-brown color until reaching sexual maturity. Thanks to their stick-like appearance, immature lizards are difficult to detect on the tree branches.

Brookesinae are seldom seen, and these tiny chameleonids are considered rare by many people. In reality, many species are not uncommon; they are merely superbly camou-

Brookesia peyrierasi, one of the smallest vetebrates on Earth.

[1] E.-R. Brygoo, "*Faune de Madagascar, Sauriens Chamaeleonides. Genre Chamaeleo,*" vol. 33, CNRS-ORSTOM: 1971.

Chapter 4
Elements of Chameleonid Biology

Origins

The genus *Mimeosaurus*, extinct for 65 million years, is believed to be one of the ancestors of the modern-day chameleonids. The oldest distinctly chameleonid-like fossil known is *Chamaeleo intermedius*. Study of the bone structure of *C. intermedius* showed it to have been much like that of today's *C. namaquensis*. *C. intermedius* lived in the Kenyan savannas 14 million years ago, during the Miocene epoch.

The Cradle of the Chameleonids

Whether continental Africa or the island of Madagascar was the point of origin of the chameleonids is still at issue. However, the phylogenetic link between the agamids and the

The External Anatomy of Chameleonids

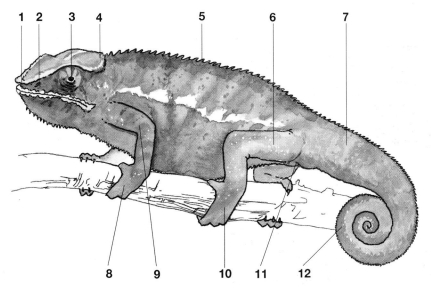

1. Mouth
2. Nostril
3. Eye
4. Frill
5. Dorsal spines
6. Hind leg
7. Base of tail
8. Forefoot
9. Foreleg
10. Hind foot
11. Vent
12. Tail

Chamaeleo cristatus (male). Females are greener than the males, but both sexes have very short tails.

chameleonids has been established. Since no agamid lizards are found in Madagascar, the theory that chameleons originated there seems untenable.

D. Hillenius[1] defended the theory of African origin, with east Africa being the point of the chameleonids' dispersal. He based his defense on the fact that in Africa chameleonids exhibit the largest number of morphological differences. Additional evidence is provided by the fact that chameleonid fossils have been found in Kenya but not in Madagascar.

It is my opinion also that Africa is the cradle of the chameleonids. It remains to be seen how these animals dispersed and diversified. Paleogeography, the study of pollens, and genetics may allow us someday to reconstruct the scenario. We know that over several thousand years the climate went from periods of cold (the Ice Ages)

to periods that were much warmer.

Since the plains were milder and the level of the oceans lower during glacial periods, the chameleonids that pursued a warmer climate moved across ever longer distances as they sought new habitats. When the climate warmed, certain chameleonids were obliged to seek the cooler environment they needed by colonizing higher altitudes. Other chameleon species became confined to islands such as the Seychelles, Madagascar, and Bioko Island. There, separated from their original groups, they thrived and speciated in the shelter of the forest. I believe that chameleonids originally moved onto the island of Madagascar while it was linked to Africa. This was about 20 million years ago, before the appearance of highly evolved mammals.

The Strange Anatomy of the Chameleonids

Chameleonids have no trouble hiding. Just when you think you are going to capture one, it disappears in a flurry among the tree branches, slipping though the boughs into the foliage.

Believing themselves threatened, they sometimes let themselves fall to the ground, where, uninjured, they hurry away. Alternatively, they drop to a lower perch where they secure themselves with their prehensile tail and grasping feet. In this latter position they safely remain while the predator searches in vain under the tree.

Skull

The chameleonid's skull is equipped with rudimentary, identical teeth, which are attached to the bone. This type of dentition, known as acrodont, refers to the fact that the teeth are unsocketed.

Legs and Tail

Of all the arboreal lizards, only chameleonids have developed such thick limbs and such a strong grip. Some authors have noticed that certain large species—such as *Chamaeleo j. johnstoni*—that live in habitats subject to high winds possess proportionally larger and more muscular limbs and grasping feet.[2] This observation is interesting because it indicates that the chameleonids have adapted to specific climatic conditions.

To grasp branches securely, chameleonids have five toes on each foot, fused in opposing groups to form "pincers." The front feet have two toes joined on the outside and three joined on the inside. In the back feet that arrangement is reversed. All the toes bear claws (bifid in members of the genus *Rhampholeon*). In addition, the inside of the feet and the tip of the tail are equipped with cone-like scales,[3] rather like the non-skid surface of stair treads. It has long been noted that the tails of

Chamaeleo balteatus (male) showing acrodont dentition.

arboreal chameleons are somewhat flattened laterally and strongly prehensile. It seems that canopy species (*C. oweni*, etc.) have the longest tails (proportionally). Chameleons that inhabit lower levels have proportionally shorter tails (*C. cristatus*, etc.). Why is this? Both *C. oweni* and *C. cristatus* are found in the same equatorial forest in central Africa, but they occupy very different niches. Perhaps the long tail (up to one and a half times its body length) offers the heliophilic (sun-loving) *C. oweni* a more secure grip on exposed sunning areas.

On the other hand, *C. cristatus*, a lower-level (undergrowth) specialist

not subjected to gusty winds (hence not needing as strong a grip on its perch), has a tail only one half its body length. *C. cristatus*, a lover of coolness and high humidity, is said to be a sciophilous (shade-loving) species. Madagascar's *C. balteatus*, another canopy species, also possesses a remarkably long tail. Although we may speculate on the relationship between the length of the tail and the chameleons' behavior, at the moment such thoughts remain just that—speculation. Further studies on the relationship between tail length and preferred habitat need to be done.

Skeleton and Muscular System

The chameleonid's adaptation to a tree-dwelling life has brought about certain anatomical changes: cartilaginous ribs allow harmless falls; grasping "hands" provide a sure grip, even during high winds; highly specialized hyoid muscles in the extensible tongue allow very successful insect hunting. Specialized eye musculature permits independent eye motion and ensures that neither enemies nor prey escape notice. The spinal column is capable of considerable flexure.

Digestive System

Although chameleonids are largely insectivorous, they also consume some plant material.

Their small, conical teeth are used mainly for holding their prey. The tongue is a fleshy extensor muscle covering a cartilaginous core that is fixed onto a mobile bone and to which hyoid muscles are attached. Under a microscope, the organ shows small hooks and rings on its surface that assist in the retention of prey.

The mouth contains mucus-secreting glands and glands that produce a non-sticky saliva of variable viscosity.

The digestive system is not highly specialized; the stomach, which is essentially tubular, secretes extremely active enzymes and hydrochloric acid. The intestine is short and ends at the cloaca—the multipurpose cavity used for feces and urine and as a passageway during delivery of the young or egg deposition. Other organs that are annexed to the digestive system and that help in the process are the liver and the pancreas.

Respiratory and Circulatory Systems

The chameleonid's blood volume represents 3 percent of the animal's total body weight. The blood is relatively low in red blood cells. The immune system relies upon lymphocytes, monocytes, plasmacytes, and antibodies.

Like other animals, the chameleon can breathe either through its nose or through its mouth. The palate is perforated by a pair of sinuses allowing passage of air from the nostrils through the choanal slit, then into the lungs. Air taken in by the mouth passes through the larynx and the glottal sphincter, which is behind the tongue, into the trachea and from there into the lungs. As the ambient temperature rises, both the volume of the air moved and the respiratory rate increase. This not only boosts the oxygen level, but helps dissipate the body heat of the animal.

The paired lungs may be simple (unilobed), or the lobes may be subdivided into two lobes (bilobed). The lung structure is used by some researchers in the taxonomic process to differentiate between species. *Chamaeleo oustaleti* and *Brookesia* have simple lungs, while most other *Chamaeleo* species have bilobed lungs.

The lungs contain only a few alveoli (blood vessel-lined sacs where oxygen is taken in and carbon dioxide given off). Lungs with relatively few alveoli are limited in the amount of oxygen transfer that can take place at a given time.

The heart is three chambered, with two atria supplying the single ventricle. In the heart, venous and arterial blood mix, which again lim-

This dissection of a *Chamaeleo jacksonii xantholophus* (female) shows the lungs, intestinal tract, and ovules.

its the amount of oxygenated blood reaching the organs.

Urinary and Genital Systems

The urinary passages are distinct from the generative canals, although both lead to the cloaca. The feces and urine, excreted together as droppings, consist largely of urate solids suspended in a transparent jelly-like fluid.

Both male and female chameleons have paired gonads, situated near the kidneys. The female has two oviducts, which serve as a uterus. The male has two erectile hemipenes that are located in the tail behind the cloaca.

Nervous System

Chemeleonids have a well-developed nervous system. The brain has left and right hemispheres, which are quite distinct from each other. There are twelve pairs of cranial nerves.

Changing Colors

Physiology: This phenomenon is the result of two factors acting on the skin's specialized color cells. One is physical, called the Tyndall effect (the scattering of light by particles suspended in a liquid or gas; e.g., a street light seen on a foggy night); the other is neuro-hormonal.

Seen under the microscope, a chameleonid's skin consists of an upper level, the epidermis, and a lower level, the dermis. The epidermis is made up of a layer of transparent, hardened cells, under which are cells that have not yet hardened (the Malpighian layer). The Malpighian layer contains guanocytes—cells

(left)
Chamaeleo minor (female).

(right)
Chamaeleo minor (female) showing warning coloration.

How Chameleonids Change Color

Pigment	Coloring Effect	Cells
Melanin (protein)	Darkening: black, blue violet	Melanophores
Guanine (protein)	Lightening: white	Guanocytes
Carotenoids (fat and oil)	Red, brown, yellow, orange	Xanthophores
Purines	Tyndall effect	Iridocytes

that appear yellow against a light background and blue against an opaque background. If we put a piece of chameleon skin on a glass slide, illuminated from below, the skin appears yellow; if we close the diaphragm of the microscope, the skin appears blue.

Between the dermis and epidermis are refractive cells called iridocytes. These cells, which are responsible for the Tyndall effect, diffuse only part of the sunlight reaching them. Depending on the position of the iridocytes, the light might pass up through the transparent dead cells of the epidermis, or it might penetrate farther down into the skin mass to affect the other color cells.

Deeper in the skin are the chromatophores—contractile cells containing pigment. As these cells contract, the colors become visible through the dermis. The action of the different chromatophores—the erythrophores, which contain red pigment; the melanophores, which contain dark brown or black pigment; and the xanthophores, which contain yellow pigment—in combi-

nation with the iridocytes can produce a dizzying array of colors on the chameleonid's skin.

The chromatophores are subject to a neuro-hormonal influence. The hormone, intermidin, acts on the large sympathetic nerve, which then initiates the contraction or relaxation of the chromatophore cells.

Large, bright spots appear on the rostrum of *Chamaeleo gallus* when it sees a female. The female's response, which can occur in two seconds, is a display of little blue dots on her snout.

Chamaeleo bifidus (female) molting.

The iridocytes allow more light to penetrate the skin, the skin colors darken, and the animal flattens its body to provide greater surface area for light absorption.

The chromatic cells are divided into three distinct layers, which successively show the yellow, black, brown, or red colors as one goes deeper into the dermis. The carotenoid pigments are often joined to the protein pigments, and this modifies the colors even more.

Significance: Highly colored liveries are characteristic of sexually mature chameleonids. Young chameleonids show dull colors: gray, beige, dark brown. Their lack of color intensity, due to physiological (hormonal) factors, results in effective camouflage. Color also indicates an animal's state of health.

With the beginning of sexual activity, and under the influence of the sex hormones as well as other chemical messengers such as adrenaline and acetylcholine, the pigment-containing cells enlarge and the chameleonids' behavior changes. The males become more territorial, sometimes aggressive, and occasionally are very active sexually. When males meet one another, color changes can display intent—be it aggressive, submissive, or sexual. Color intensification also appears to attract chameleonids to gather for the purpose of reproduction.

Skin

The permeability of the skin varies with the habitat of the particular

When at rest, the chromatophores lie under the dermis and the iridocytes diffuse the light back through the guanocytes in the epidermis. The skin appears pale yellow, green, and even white. When the chameleon is annoyed, the iridocytes move, light diffuses to the dermis, and the erythrophores contract; the animal displays vivid warning colors and assumes a threatening attitude. When the lizard is active and unthreatened, the iridocytes move again, light is diffused to the dermis, and the xanthophores and melanophores contract to show beautiful colors. The patterns become brighter.

Color can also play a role when the chameleonid is cold and needs to increase its body temperature.

species. In the desert, chameleonids are protected from desiccation by a thick, dry skin. Mountain species, however, have a thinner skin that is more permeable to moisture.

The scalation of each species is unique. The scalation may be homogeneous (*C. deremensis*); heterogeneous (*Bradypodion p. pumilum*); finely pearled (*C. chamaeleon*); rough (*Rhampholeon kerstenii*); or even velvety (*C. willsii*).

Chameleonids do not shed their skins in one piece as do snakes and some other lizards, but rather exfoliate in patches. Shedding occurs more frequently during times of rapid growth and less frequently when growth is slow. The epidermis cracks along the borders between the scales, or squama, then separates from the newly formed skin beneath. The old pieces dry up and harden, then flake off.

The shedding process can take a number of days, but it is vital that it be completed. When shreds of skin fail to shed, the chameleon attempts to rub them off on branches. Since flaking skin on the eyelids and snout may impair vision, the chameleon tries to remove them as quickly as possible. Should some dead skin remain, the area between the layers of skin becomes a prime breeding ground for bacteria. Bacterial growth degrades the dead skin and permanently damages the epidermis.

Unlike snakes, chameleonids continue to eat normally just before shedding. Once the dead skin has completely flaked off, the lizard again appears bright and sleek.

About the Senses

We know that chameleonids have at least the five senses familiar to us all. It is only through the receptive organs and intermediary nerves that the brain can perceive and analyze the world. The chameleonid's faculties should be studied individually: hearing, sight, smell, taste, and touch—including thermic sensitivity. Finally, the parietal eye may provide a sixth sense—sensitivity to certain light rays.

Sight

Chameleonids have binocular vision; their eyes move independently of each other and in any direction. The eyelids cover a large

Chamaeleo willsii. Chameleonids have very keen sight, but their visual field is quite small.

part of the eye, thus providing excellent protection against desiccation (for species living in very arid regions) or against trauma. Because of the narrowness of the eyelid opening, the size of the chameleonid's visual field is very limited, but the opening provides a tight diaphragm for the pupil and very acute sight. The chameleonid's eye could be compared to a telephoto lens of 100 to 150 millimeters. This keen sight provides some compensation for the chameleonid's slowness of movement: it allows it to detect the presence of a predator, prey, or competitor, even at a distance.

When about to capture prey, the chameleonid focuses both eyes on the object to estimate the intervening

distance accurately. The loss of an eye means a corresponding loss of visual acuity and depth perception, both important considerations when capturing prey. Though some chameleonids learn to compensate for such a handicap, most do not. As a result, the tongue is not projected far enough to reach the target.

The chameleonid is able to see the range of colors from red through violet. However, the eye cannot perceive either ultraviolet or infrared. Analysis of the retina shows an absence of rods and melanin pigments necessary for nocturnal vision; therefore, the chameleonids have only diurnal vision and their activity depends on the intensity of the light.[4]

Smell and Taste

Scent and taste are analyzed by the Jacobson's organ, a pair of cavities on the anterior medial palate. These organs, which contain sensitive cells covered by thin mucus, are activated by the first cranial nerve.

Particles brought into the mouth by the tongue inform the chameleonid of the odor and taste of its prey.

One often sees a male chameleonid rubbing his cloaca on branches to deposit secretions that soon dry in place. These secretions provide chemical messages for other chameleonids, who pick up the scent to be interpreted. In this way the chameleonids know if they are on a branch marked as the territory of another chameleonid. (This behavior is not known in stump-tailed chameleons.)

Chameleonids exhibit decided food preferences. In fact, they have long been recognized as picky eaters. If given a good choice of prey (grasshoppers, flies, spiders, mealworms, snails, stinkbeetles), they quickly identify and pursue what they like best. If several chameleonids are in the same enclosure, fights for the preferred prey will ensue.

Hearing

The chameleonid's ear has simplified over time; it is not visible externally. This has led many authors to conclude, rather hastily, that chameleonids are deaf. In fact, chameleonids have neither an exterior aperture nor a tympanic membrane. Parts of the internal ear are also absent—the oval "window" and the perilymphatic bag that leads to the external part of the ordinary ear. But the presence of fluid in the "snail" and of tissue that acts as a tympanic membrane

Bradypodion pumilum (female).

enables chameleonids to detect frequencies from 200 to 600 Hz. Some authors claim that the level of sensitivity depends on the individual specimen studied; the montane species (*C. j. jacksonii*, or *C. höhnelii*) do not seem to hear as well as the lowland forms.[5]

Females of *C. oweni* and *C. johnstoni* are known to make low "purring" sounds when held by a human or when approached by a potential mate. But studies have yet to determine whether the male can hear these vibrations.

Touch and Thermal Sensitivity

The parts most sensitive to touch are the corners of the lips, the area along the spinal column, the flanks, and the tip of the tail.

Chameleons (but not stump-tailed species) are attracted to any

Chamaeleo gracilis (female).

source of heat. This was confirmed by British scientist B. R. Burrage, who measured the temperature of the substrate upon which South African *Bradypodion* slept. Burrage then proceeded to measure the temperature of the nearby surroundings. He found that the ground under the chameleonids was, on the average, 1.8 to 3.6°F (1–2°C) higher than the rest of the ground.[6]

Sensitivity to Light Rays

Over a century ago, French scientist Paul Bert showed that,

The Parietal Eye

1. Nerve
2. Skin
3. Bone
4. Pineal organ
5. Paraphysis
6. Brain

Parietal Eye

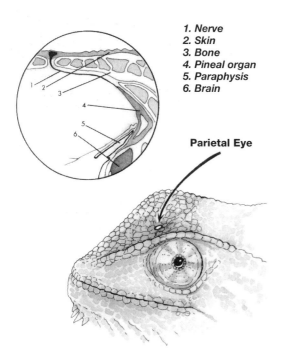

whether the chameleonid is asleep or awake, blue and violet rays produce a strong reaction on its chromatophores, whereas red and yellow rays have no influence.[7]

It is obvious the light quality and quantity affect the chamelenoid's mood. When I started to keep chameleonids, I exposed a *Chamaeleo gracilis gracilis* female to light from a normal incandescent bulb. The light of these bulbs is unbalanced, being too poor in certain wave lengths to approximate the quality of sunlight. Specifically, spectrographic analysis shows a large proportion of red and yellow rays and a small proportion of blue, violet, and green. The chameleon changed from her normal bright green to dirty yellow in the space of about ten days and remained this color regardless of her mood. I decided to expose her again to daylight, after which her beautiful green color slowly came back, becoming stable after a month. Can we explain why?

Chameleonids, like many other reptiles, are endowed with a most fascinating organ—the parietal eye. The parietal eye is known in the New Zealand sphenodon as the "third eye." It is found in many lizards between the other two eyes, sometimes (in chameleonids) covered with scales, sometimes (in iguanids) not. This eye is light-sensitive, but it reacts only to the most energetic light rays—those responsible for our awareness of blue and violet. This organ is linked to the autonomic nervous system, which controls involuntary activities in all vertebrates. Although much research remains to be done, it seems highly probable that the parietal eye plays a vital role in regulating the chameleonid's biological cycles.[8]

Chamaeleo minor. **The parietal eye, which is quite small in chameleonids, is usually not visible externally.**

[1]D. Hillenius, "Differentiation within the genus *Chamaeleo.*" *Notes on Chameleons,* Beaufortia, 8, pp. 1–92: 1959.

____, "Comparative cytology: aids and new complications in chameleon taxonomy." *ibid.*, Beaufortia, 9, pp. 201–218: 1963.

[2]S. C. Halfpenny, "The Care and Breeding of *C. johnstoni* in Captivity." *British Herpetological Society Bulletin*, no. 39: 1992.

[3]M. Schuster, "*Experimentelle Untersuchungen zum Beutefang, Kampf und Fortpflanzungsverhalten von Chamaeleo jacksonii*" (Ph.D. dissertation, Münster University): 1979.

[4]A. Rochon-Duvigneaud, "*Le chameleon et son oeil.*" *Annales occulistes:* 1933.

[5]E. Glenn Wever, *The Reptile Ear, Its Structure and Functions.* Princeton University Press: 1978.

[6]B. R. Burrage, "Comparative ecology and behavior of *Chamaeleon pumilis pumilis* and *C. namaquensis.*" *Sauria, Chamaeleontidae:* 1973.

[7]P. Bert, "*Influence de la lumière sur les êtres vivants.*" *Revue Scientifique*: 1878.

[8]P. J. Regal, "Temperature and light requirements of captive reptiles." *SSAR* No. 1: 1980.

Chapter 5
Physiology and Behavior

Rest and Activity

Like all biological activity, the activity patterns of chameleonids have rhythmic cycles. Some cycles, such as day length, are rather simple. Others, such as seasonal changes, like the revolutions of the earth and the moon and solar activity, are more complex. The lives of the various chameleonids are affected by all these phenomena. Not only are chameleons diurnal creatures (active by day and sleeping at night), but the activity patterns of most species are greatly affected by the seasons.

Thermoregulation

Because the chameleonid is a cold-blooded (poikilothermic) creature, its body temperature is critically affected by the environment. Poikilotherms have no internal body-temperature regulating mechanisms. When their bodies cool below a certain internal temperature, hypothermia occurs and enzyme action is reduced. Conversely, when overheated, hyperthermia can result in cell damage, and enzyme action is also impeded. Either condition can prove fatal. Thus, the metabolic functions and the very life of any poikilotherm depend on its ability to maintain a suitable body temperature by utilizing external stimuli.

In their environments chameleonids do not always encounter ideal temperatures. Some days can be very cool while others may be

Chamaeleo jacksonii xantholophus (female) resting.

hot and dry. Thus it is necessary for chameleons, like other lizards, to utilize their morphological characteristics to regulate their body temperature.[1]

A cold chameleonid can increase its body temperature by several degrees by positioning itself in the sunlight, darkening its color, and modifying the volume of air contained in its lungs. Conversely, a warm chameleonid can reduce its body temperature by moving into the shade, lightening its body color, and panting. Not only is absorption of heat reduced, but moisture evaporation from the mucous membranes of the mouth, throat, primary digestive tract, and respiratory tract can actually cool the lizard. In these ways chameleonids are able to maintain their body temperatures within the necessary parameters, and often they may actually attain the optimum temperature needed

for their functioning: the preferred body temperature, or PBT. PBT varies by species, specimen, age, gender, and level of activity.

Light Quality

The amount and quality of the sun's radiant energy that reaches the atmosphere do not change. But on their way to the ground the rays go through disturbed air strata and are more or less diffused by clouds and particulates.

The position of any given portion of the earth's surface relative to the sun also affects the amount and quality of the radiant energy it receives. Thus, both temperature and the wave length of the ambient light vary with the time of day and the season of the year. At dawn, for example, the shorter-waved rays (blues and violets) weaken, thereby enhancing the longer-waved rays, which give the sky and sun a red

coloration. In winter, or when there are many clouds in the sky, the same short-waved rays, which are believed to be responsible for the stimulation of the parietal eye of the lizard, also weaken.

Lizards endowed with a parietal eye have been shown to be more active under the exposure of violet rays (Palenschat, 1964; Moehn, 1974); they eat and move more. The balance and the quality of light, which change with the seasons, thus produce profound effects on the behavior of lizards.

Rest

Chameleonid species that live in regions where adverse seasonal temperatures are experienced have developed methods of protecting themselves while awaiting moderating temperatures. Two such methods are hibernation and aestivation.

The term *hibernation* pertains to winter dormancy, *aestivation* to summer dormancy.

Species of chameleons that hibernate are those from high altitudes and subtropical regions, areas that can and usually do experience a significant drop in winter temperatures. Conversely, tropical lowland chameleonids may aestivate during periods of excessively high temperatures or during prolonged drought.

In both cases the lizards usually burrow in yielding soils, mosses, or other substrates, or take cover beneath leaves or debris. Certain species spend the winter, or a part of it, clinging to branches.

I was able to observe some chameleonids (*Chamaeleo parsonii*, *Bradypodion p. pumilum*) that spent part or all of the austral (southern) winter clinging to a tree branch; others, such as *Brookesia superciliaris*, *Chamaeleo campani*, and *Bradypodion damaranum,* either took refuge beneath a pile of dead leaves or burrowed into the ground to hibernate.

Chameleonids generally rest during the dry season. In equatorial zones the dry seasons correspond to the periods of highest temperatures. In tropical zones the dry seasons correspond to cooler periods. The increase/decrease in temperature, in combination with a significant decrease in humidity, cues the chameleonids that it is time for a period of rest. Both hibernation and aestivation may last several weeks.

To sum up, both hibernation and aestivation are triggered by decreasing humidity and adverse temperatures.

Activity

We saw earlier that chameleonids are diurnal animals that stop all activity with diminishing light levels. It is probable that the activity patterns of chameleonids are also influenced by the intensity of light rays. The number of hours of sunlight per day (absolute heliophany, or A.H.) influences chameleons as well. While at the equator day length is a constant 12 hours throughout the year, in tropical regions the length of the day varies according to the season. This variation becomes greater with an increase in latitude. Day length may vary from 10 hours and 50 minutes to 13 hours and 20 minutes near 20 degrees latitude North. Total solar energy is greatest in tropical regions.

The activity patterns of many chameleonids are directly related to the climate. These lizards are most active with the return of moderate temperatures and rain. While in tropical areas the rains signify warmth and humidity, equatorial rains produce cool climatic conditions.

In Tananarive, Madagascar, *Chamaeleo lateralis* ends its hibernation with the onset of the moderating temperatures associated with the first rains of September. At that time the entire chameleon population around this city emerges from hiding places and again takes up residence in the bushes. In combination with the prolonged rest of hibernation, the climatic changes also stimulate sexual activity by the lizards.

Hunting

"I have seen chameleons here, but how often do they say in our country that they don't eat? Just the same, I have seen their tongues catch flies, draw them in and eat them." (W. Lodewijcksz.)

The keen vision of chameleonids allows them to lie in wait for their prey. Once spotted and deemed edible, the prey is captured with the extensible tongue.

It is the hyoid muscles that enable the chameleonid to whip out its tongue, trap the victim, and pull it back into the mouth. The tongue's highly efficient contractile muscle is folded back on itself like an accordion. Discs (which bear the picturesque name of "Z-discs") inserted throughout the muscle fiber allow maximum contraction. In some species the tongue, when fully extended, exceeds the length of the chameleon's body (*Chamaeleo oweni*, *Brookesia superciliaris*).

In 1966 Ogilvie observed *Chamaeleo höhnelii* rubbing the sides of their snouts against branches.[2] This movement, which he called "jaw wiping," was also noticed by Bourgat in *C. pardalis* and other species. Ogilvie supposed that the chamel-

Chamaeleo minor juvenile (male) in cornflowers.

besides insects—vertebrates (lizards, frogs, birds, and small mammals) and snails are regularly consumed by some chameleons.

R. M. Bourgat has found vegetable debris in the stomach contents of one third of *C. pardalis*.[3] Other authors testify to having seen chameleons occasionally eat leaves and even fruit and French fries! They do not say whether the animals ate these items voluntarily or were force fed. Personally, I have seen young chameleons eating cornflower leaves of their own free will on a number of occasions. Invariably, they bite into the vegetation like an herbivorous reptile, tear it, and swallow the piece. Chameleons have also been observed eating earth, probably to get minerals they required.

Dietary Needs

Although the diets of chameleonids vary by species, within each species the quantity, size, and quality of food items are determined by the size of the individual. Females and growing young have a great need for minerals and proteins. Lacking them, chameleonids confront numerous physical ailments. Small vertebrates, snails, and slugs all contain both calcium and protein, hence are important dietary items. Insects also contain both, but usually in lesser amounts.

Young chameleonids have voracious appetites, but most nutrients are used to sustain rapid growth rates. A growing chameleonid may

eons were leaving some kind of attractive secretion to draw the flies on which they feed. It is also possible that this behavior was a way of marking their territories.

I have observed chameleons using their forepaws to help manipulate large prey items. Such items may also be captured, partially immobilized, dropped, then recaptured with the tongue. This behavior is most frequently observed in *C. quadricornis* and *C. minor*.

Nutrition

Chameleonids are carnivorous insectivores. Analyses of their stomach contents and fresh droppings, as well as on-the-spot observations, disclose that,—

eat up to 20 percent of its body weight in food each day. Certain species show a particular preference for one type of insect. It appears that these acquired preferences are influenced by the food supply in the surroundings.

Defense and Territoriality

Chameleonids rely on one or several ploys when faced by an enemy:
- immobilization reflex (stump-tailed chameleons)
- concealment
- retreat
- jumping
- bluff
- biting

When disturbed at night chameleonids sometimes drop from their

branches, falling to the ground, where they then hiss and breathe noisily. In 1974 S. R. Parcher dubbed this behavior "nocturnal predation response."[4]

Chamaeleo owenii juvenile (male) opening his mouth and hissing.

Chameleonids are territorial creatures of habit. I have seen them retire to the very same sleeping tree every night. The young animals that I have observed in the wild seem less territorial than the adults, which select and defend a given area. The size of this area depends directly on the abundance of prey. The territory of an adult chameleonid can include about 400 square feet (several dozen square meters).

Reproduction

There is no doubt that vision plays a major role in chameleonids' interactions. Whether vision alone or vision in combination with other

Chamaeleo quadricornis (male) in an intimidating posture: the gular crest is deployed, the barbs are bristling, and the coloration is hightened.

Chamaeleo oustaleti standing like a Masai warrior with his spear.

senses is employed by the males to distinguish females of their own species from other, similar, ones is not known with certainty.

Only rarely do two morphologically similar species share identical habitats in the wild. However, that is often not the case in captivity, where we have kept very similar species together. Among these were *C. willsii* and young *C. minor*. Our observations were quite interesting.

In an attempt to induce hybridization, we caged sexually mature young *C. minor* females with sexually active *C. willsii* males. Nothing happened. We then reversed the pairing, caging young *C. minor* males with adult *C. willsii* females. Again nothing happened. But when sexes of the same species were caged together, normal reactions—including breeding—occurred.

Of the two sexes, male chameleonids are the more aggressive and territorial. Intricate head motions are among the cues used by males to define and defend their territories. However, it seems that coloration and pattern are the most important factors in chameleonid communication, and the meanings are readily interpreted by specimens of both sexes within given populations. Color and pattern changes are used extensively both in territoriality displays and in advertising sexual receptivity (or lack of it). Colors, patterns, and appendages (horns, crests) are species-specific.

Through head motions, adult male chameleonids advertise their presence to potential rivals. The approach of an interloping mature male causes other actions as well: rapid intensification of color and pattern, inflation of the body, and flaring of neck flaps. However, it is only the adult males of the same species that interact and display in these ways. If an adult male approaches an immature male of the same species, a male of another species, or a sexually receptive female of either his own or another species, his approach and displays are likely to be studiously ignored. This lack of reaction may lead the adult male to think he has met a sexually receptive female, and an attempt at breeding may ensue. I was able to observe a *C. pardalis* male attempting to mate with a young *C. brevicornis* and another attempted copulation between a male *C. dilepis* and a young male *C. johnstoni*.

Courtship

A male chameleonid begins the courtship ritual with rhythmic head movements including both up-and-down and side-to-side motions. He may indulge in up to eight side-to-side motions and as many, or more, vertical nods. A receptive female who has recognized a potential male usually remains passive, but may at times respond to the male's nodding by gently undulating her body as she clings to the branch.

I have noticed that some male *C. johnstoni* and *C. oweni* emit a low "groaning" (see page 25) while courting a female. When the male is producing this sound, gentle vibrations may be felt if he is touched. It is possible that the females are sensitive to these sounds or vibrations and react to them.

When the female is receptive she remains quiet and displays passive colors. She will be joined by the male, who will pursue her should she change position. If the female remains receptive to his advances the male will mount her, contorting

Chamaeleo oustaleti (male and female) mating. The hemipenes can be seen in the photo at the bottom of the page.

Embryonic Development

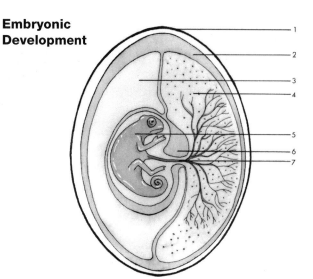

1. Shell
2. Chorion
3. Allantois
4. Vitellus
5. Embryo
6. Endoplast
7. Umbilical cord

Seasons and Sexual Activity

In equatorial regions and certain parts of tropical regions, reproduction may take place at any time of year. However, seasonal weather changes play an indispensable part in inducing sexual activity.

In his thesis on *Chamaeleo pardalis*, R. M. Bourgat points out that "during periods of sexual activity, the density of the known populations increases, and little groups form."[5] I believe it is possible that at these times the rapidly growing young chameleons, having attained larger sizes and more brilliant coloration, are more easily noticed.

Fertilization and Egg Laying

In its transformation to an egg, the fertilized ovule passes into the glandular portion of the oviduct, becoming coated with different secretions on its journey. The embryo is surrounded by yolk, albumen, an egg membrane, and a shell. In addition, the egg has embryonic extensions such as amnion, allontois, and the umbilical vesicle. The eggshells of the typical chameleons (*Chamaeleo* species) are more flexible and leathery than those of the stump-

his body until the cloacae of the pair are aligned. A blood-engorged hemipenis is inserted into the female's cloaca, with actual copulation lasting from three to 10 minutes. Upon completion the male withdraws the now flaccid hemipenis and releases his mate, who changes her color to indicate that she is no longer receptive and moves away. Following a successful mating, if the female is approached by a courting male, she displays warning colors and utilizes threatening postures to dissuade him.

Hutching Success					
Clutch	Eggs	Eaten	Infertile	Died	Hatched
1	12	3	2		7
2	6	2			4
3	14	3		2	9
4	13			2	11
5	15	2	3		10

tailed species (*Rhampholeon* and *Brookesia*). However, the shells of all are water- and gas-permeable.

The yolk is the source of nutrition and energy for the embryo. The yolk is rich in calcium, which the embryo uses for the growth of its skeleton.

Ovoviviparous species retain eggs without calcareous shells in the oviducts until the young are ready to come into the world. Thermoregulation by the mother permits the correct development of the embryo.

In oviparous species, the eggs develop in the enlarged portion of the oviduct, which plays a role similar to that of the mammalian uterus. Eggs are laid, in more or less embryonic form, an average of one to two months after mating. Incubation times can be quite variable.

Egg Laying (Oviposition)

Gravid oviparous females must come to earth to find a suitable nesting spot. Soil temperature and suitable dampness are important considerations. If possible, female chameleons dig their nests in a clearing next to shrubs or grass. Occasionally we have disturbed females digging in the middle of fields. They then abandoned even nearly completed nests to go elsewhere and start again.

Female chameleons use all four feet in digging. The hole is usually shallow, although deeper nests have been observed where the substrate is especially soft.

Depending on the species as well as the size and age of the female, from three to 60 eggs may be laid. The eggs are sometimes

Chamaeleo oustaleti laying her eggs. This usually occurs about 30 days after copulation.

The exhausted female after she has laid all of her eggs.

A clutch of incubating *Chamaeleo wiedersheimi* eggs.

branches, allowing the newborns to break free and gain easy access to twigs in their arboreal habitat. Stillbirths are rare; when they occur in captive chameleons, this may indicate that the mother's diet has lacked protein and calcium.

Most species of chameleons are oviparous. Embryonic development depends on three factors:

- temperature
- humidity (moisture content) of the substrate or atmosphere
- stage of development of the embryo at the time of laying

Egg development can be slowed by a drop in substrate temperature or humidity. Eggs of certain tropical species go through a dry and cold/hot and humid diapause (delay or cessation of development) during their incubation and have lengthy incubation durations (up to 16 months). For example, the eggs of *C. lateralis*, laid just prior to the cold season (around May), sustain a dia-

connected by a thin membrane. After oviposition the female chameleon fills the hole as completely as possible and attempts to obliterate external signs of nesting.

Both genera of the forest-dwelling stump-tailed chameleon lay their eggs (two on average) beneath decomposing leaves and forest litter.

Development of the Embryos and Live Birth

Parturition in ovoviviparous chameleonids (*Bradypodion* species and some East African *Chemeleo* species) occurs some four to seven months after mating. The number of babies born is between six and 30, depending on the age and the species of the female. At birth the babies are enclosed in a thin, transparent membrane that is somewhat adhesive externally. Rather than dropping to the ground, this membranous sac adheres to leaves or

A hatching egg. (The coin in the photo is slightly smaller than an American dime.)

pause of several months before beginning normal development in September, when mild weather returns to their Madagascan homeland. However, when kept at an average temperature of 71 to 74°F (21.5–23.5°C) the majority of eggs hatch after four or five months. Since the eggs are laid in more or less advanced embryonic condition, average figures for hatching times are approximate.

Depending on the species and its habitat, the eggs deposited can be in either an early or an advanced stage of development. The number of eggs laid is always inverse to the eggs' embryonic stage.

While observing stump-tailed chameleons (*Brookesia thieli, B. superciliaris, Rhampholeon s. spectrum*) André Peyrieras and I found that eggs kept between 72 and 75°F (22–24°C) almost always hatch three weeks after being laid. Conversely, for species that lay

many eggs (*C. chameleon, C. calyptratus*), incubation lasts several months.

During the final weeks chameleonid eggs swell until they may be twice as large as when first laid. As the egg nears the end of the incubation period the permeable shell stretches and becomes mottled with darker areas. Interior pressure increases and albumen seeps out. After pipping, the baby within the egg often protrudes its head but (usually) does not fully emerge until the remaining yolk is fully absorbed (which may require another day or two).

Temperature-determined Sex Ratios

It is not certain whether the incubation temperature of chameleonid eggs plays as significant a role in determining sex as it does in other groups of reptiles. Certainly it is an important consideration in the sex determination of some chelonians

Chamaeleo höhnelli emerging from its birth sac. The females of ovoviviparous species sometimes eat immediately after giving birth, but the young are never devoured.

When the egg is laid, the shell is tough and firm. As the embryo develops, the shell softens and the egg swells.

Chamaeleo parsonii cristifer juvenile.

(turtles), some geckos, and all crocodilians.

Initially, we are inclined to discount the role of temperature in determining the sex of embryo chameleons. However, we do feel it must be addressed in the case of *C. parsonii*.

The incubation of *C. parsonii* eggs is among the longest known for a lizard. In the wild, incubation of the eggs of this species may last 19 months. The long duration may be explained by the fact that from laying to hatching the substrate temperature does not vary much from a cool 63° to 72°F (17°–21°C). We have found a two-to-one sex ratio, females being favored, in these clutches. However, that ratio may be entirely natural for the species. In other high-altitude species, among them *C. lateralis, C. quadricornis,* and *C. fischeri tavetanus*, the ratio of males and females is equal. Obvi-

ously, controlled testing would be required before firm conclusions could be drawn.

Comments on Hatching Success

In the wild, the eggs of chameleonids are subject to predation by ants and other egg-eating insects. Nonetheless, about half of the eggs reach full term and hatch. The babies leave the nest at the same time. An example of egg-hatching success for five clutches of *C. lateralis* follows. Clutches 2 and 5 were subject to an austral (southern) winter.

Growth of Young Chameleonids

Young chameleonids grow quickly. Given an abundance of food and suitable climatic conditions, they thrive. As with all reptiles, growth continues throughout their lives but slows with advancing age or when conditions become less favorable.

[1]R. B. Cowles and C. M. Bogert, "A preliminary study of the thermal requirements of desert reptiles." 1944.
[2]P. W. Ogilvie, "An anatomical and behavioral investigation of a previously undescribed pouch found in certain species of genus *Chamaeleo*." Ph.D. dissertation, Abstract, B, USA 27 (6) 2 194: 1966.
[3]R. M. Bourgat, "*Recherches écologiques et biologiques sur le* Chamaeleo pardalis *de l'île de la Réunion et de Madagascar*." Dissertation, Montpellier, 1969.
[4]S. R. Parcher, "Observations on the Natural History of Six Malagasy Chamaeleontidae." *Z. Tierpsychology*, 34, 500–523: 1974.
[5]R. M. Bourgat, *op. cit.*

Chapter 6
Population Dynamics

Climate, geography, and habitat all affect living beings.

Factors Extrinsic to Population Dynamics

The chances of survival, reproduction, and geographic extension depend on environmental factors. We will call these *factors extrinsic to population dynamics*.

Energetic Factors

Different chameleonid species have different optimum incubation temperature ranges. Too low a temperature, and the development of the embryo is obstructed. Too high a temperature, and the embryo is killed. Temperature excesses in either direction cause physiological stress in adult specimens as well.

We have seen how the quality and intensity of light influence chameleonids. By chance, I confirmed that the quality of the light changes in the course of the year. In Madagascar, I have done chromatic analyses of the solar spectrum at different times of year. In June (a cool period in southern Africa), I noticed that the solar light showed a greater proportion of red in the spectrum than usual, and thus a lesser quantity of blue rays. It is possible that these variations in light serve as a "clocking" device for the animals and initiate the hibernation process. (See page 27.)

Mechanical Factors

The most important mechanical factor directly influencing chameleonid population is fire. A forest fire can pose a direct threat to a localized species. Not only does it destroy the animals themselves, it also destroys the food sources and the top layer of soil, making egg laying difficult and proper incubation impossible. Soil erosion after the fire is another factor that affects the chameleonids. Humidity and ground and air temperature are also affected when the forest cover is destroyed.

Chemical Factors

Assuming that the chemical nature of the earth and to a larger extent the mineral and gas exchanges of the habitat affect the plants and those that feed upon them, we can say that the chemical exchanges of the habitat have an effect on chameleonid populations.

Chamaeleo brevicornis hilleniusi in its native habitat.

Analyses of the habitat soils of the Cameroon species of *C. m. montium, C. quadricornis, C. wiedersheimi, C. cristatus, C. owenii, R. s. spectrum*, and the Madagascan species *C. campani, C. lateralis, C. pardalis, C. parsonii, C. brevicornis hilleniusi, Brookesia supercilaris, B. thieli,* and *B. vadoni* showed that the sites chosen for egg deposition all had a pH of less than 6; it was less than 5 for *C. campani, C. brevicornis hillenius, B. vadoni, and R. s. spectrum*. Acid soils, which are bacteriostatic, prevent the formation and development of bacteria and fungus on the egg shells. This increases the chances of hatching.

Biotic Factors

Biotic (habitat) factors concern existing relationships between different living beings. These are complex relationships, but for the sake of simplification we shall discuss the classic relationships that exist between chameleonids and the vegetation of their habitat; and between chameleonids and other animals. We will also discuss the ways in which human intervention can modify the initial set of facts.

Predators and parasites: In nature, chameleonids pay a heavy price to predation. Their eggs are devoured by ants. The young are eaten by insects and even by other chameleonids. The adults are hunted by snakes, birds, and numerous other animals. Further, parasitism may shorten the lizards' life expectancy. The freeloaders may be ectoparasites, which live on the outside of the chameleonids (ticks and mites), or endoparasites, which live in their internal organs (roundworms, tapeworms, flukes, and filarids).

External parasites damage the skin, as do bacterial and fungal skin infections. Ticks and mites feed on the blood of their host. Another danger for chameleonids comes from biting insects such as mosquitoes, which may transmit the larvae of external and internal filarid parasites during the bite. Endoparasites may also enter the body via ingestion, through wounds, or by burrowing into the skin.

Internal parasites are classified in two categories:
- Microorganisms, including blood protozoan parasites (usually introduced by a bite from an arthropod) and bacteria (*Salmonella* sp., *Shigella* sp.), ingested by accident.
- Worms, including cestodes (flatworms and filarids), nematodes

(roundworms), and trematodes (flukes).

All parasites, whether external or internal, exploit their hosts as fully as possible in order to complete their own life cycles and reproduce. This does not, however, extend to killing the host, because the death of the host assures the death of the parasite and its potential progeny.

The amount of predation upon a chameleonid population is a limiting factor, given that there must be enough food for both parasites and their hosts. Quite logically, the chameleonid population is itself dependent upon the quantity of its food sources.

Vegetation: Chameleonids' habitats contain extremely heterogeneous vegetation, from dense forests to wooded areas. Each area has its own easily discernible sub-areas:

- Dense forests, where the tops of the trees touch, and where there is limited undergrowth. Dense forests are subdivided into dense primary mountain forests and dense primary plains forests.
- Wooded areas where the tree cover remains open and there is a carpeting of grass and other plants. Wooded areas are subdivided into degraded primary forests (called secondary forests), forest-like stretches or areas, mixed formations (where trees cover 15 to 50 percent of the ground), and wooded savannas.

Dispersion: The chameleonid population disperses only to obtain better living conditions: vegetation that assures protection against the sun, an optimal temperature range, sufficient food and water supplies.

We can identify two types of dispersion:

- Radial dispersion, where the ecological factors encourage movement in all directions around the original site.
- Linear dispersion, where the ecological conditions encourage movement in one direction only.

Any modification of the environment can influence the population dynamics.

Human activity also has an effect on the dynamics of chameleonid populations. This "anthropic factor" is illustrated by several examples:

- The natural habitat may be preserved without disturbance.
- The natural habitat may be modified through the destruction of natural resources (forest fires, agriculture, insecticides). The destruction of habitat and food supply over vast areas presents a serious threat to the local species. For species scattered over wider areas, these phenomena contribute to limiting the population dynamics.
- The habitat may be modified by felling trees in sempiternally (always) wet areas. This "soft" modification of the habitat, often the work of local farmers, seems to have helped certain chameleonid species propagate by offering them improved living conditions. In the same way, certain species do better in a degraded primary forest. Such a forest is

Chamaeleo furcifer (male). The geographical range of certain chameleons is quite small. *C. furcifer*, for example, is found only in one forest of eastern Madagascar. Breeding programs for this species are currently being considered.

richer in nourishment and ecological niches than an intact primary forest. Two species that increase in degraded forests are *C. quadricornis* and *C. pardalis*.

• Artificial geographic distribution may occur. People have introduced new chameleonid species in diverse areas, including *C. jacksonii xantholophus* in Hawaii, *C. chamaeleon* in Sicily, and *C. pardalis* in Réunion, an island in the Indian Ocean.

Chamaeleo pardalis adapts well to conditions in a degraded (transformed) forest environment.

• Hunting may be practiced. Chameleonids are sometimes harvested for the pet trade. The majority of the species subject to harvesting are spread out and generally not victims of intense hunting. Although the effect of hunting on the natural populations is thought to be minimal, over-hunting of certain localized species could threaten their survival.

Factors Intrinsic to Population Dynamics

Under the designation *factors intrinsic to population dynamics*, we will now consider the impact of certain physiological and morphological characteristics of chameleonids on the quantity of offspring.

Physiological Factors

Sexual maturity: Chameleonids reach sexual maturity at different times, depending on the climate and the species, but usually between three and nine months after birth. This rapid maturing is an economic response to normal predation; all wild species face illness, parasites, and predators. The greater the number of young that reach sexual maturity and reproduce, the more fully these losses are offset.

Fertility: Françoise Blanc hypothesized that during the reproductive cycle of *C. lateralis*, egg production is greater in rainy seasons than in dry ones. She noted, "In *Chamaeleo lateralis*, an increase in dryness during the cold season results in a delay in the first layings and probably in the reduction of the number of layings per year. It is possible that the amount of rainfall dictates the abundance of insects serving as food for the chameleons."[1]

Other species, well represented within their geographic range (*C. m. montium* in Buea, Cameroon, or *C. quadricornis* in the main mountain area of Manengouba) deposit only a small number of eggs (from three to 11 for *montium* and five to 15 for *quadricornis*) four to six times a year. These numerous layings of small quantities of eggs reflect adaptation to a favorable environment containing few predators. This gives optimum chances of growth to the young chameleonids where the climate and quantity of food remain constant throughout the year.

Ovoviviparity: Thanks to ovoviviparity, chameleonids have been

Chamaeleo lateralis major (female).

able to extend their geographic range.

Without drawing hasty conclusions, it would seem that:
- Species living in favorable habitats have fewer eggs or babies per clutch than species that dwell in more hostile habitats.
- The reproductive cycle is influenced by the climate. In a species living in a stable climate, egg laying takes place all year. The number of eggs is small and the incubation period often short. In a species having a defined "laying period," the clutches extend over the entire favorable time period and comprise a large number of eggs, usually taking several months to hatch.

Chamaeleo boettgeri.

Life expectancy: Chameleonids in their natural habitat have a relatively short life expectancy (two to four years, depending on the species). The reproductive effort is borne by the sexually precocious young animals in a heavily predatory environment. Some authors state that lizards with high reproductive efforts generally have short life spans. This shows an economic response to predatory pressures; the presence of predators leaves little chance for the species to have late reproduction, so the animals reach sexual maturity early.

In captivity, longer life spans may occur. Robert Mailloux attests to nine years for *C. jacksonii* and André Peyrieras, to seven years for *C. parsonii.*

Morphological Factors

Seminal receptacles: Saint Girons pointed out in 1962 that in the female *C. lateralis*, "seminal receptacles" were found to contain active spermatozoa. This included females that had been isolated for several months and nonetheless produced one or two fertile clutches.[2] Retention of viable sperm is known in other chameleon species as well. It allows females to "self-fertilize" and, in cases where the number of males has strongly declined, guarantees new generations and therefore a new population balance.

Secondary Sexual Characteristics: Numerous male chameleonids are adorned with diverse appendages such as nasal protrusions, horns, occipital flaps ("ears"), and crests along the spine. No one really knows the function of these appendages. During my observations of males fighting in their natural habitat, I noticed that the species that had horns used them to push their adversaries away, and that those that had crests used them to appear larger. These "feints" avoided pointless injuries or deaths. In species without these devices, a fight between males usually results in the death of the loser.

Summary

This chapter illustrates the diverse efforts of chameleonids to make the best of their environmental constraints. This adaptability has led to great diversity within the group, which is reflected in the morphology and the reproductive biology. It now appears that the chameleonids are remarkably well adapted to their ranges. Both their variety and their behavior are topics that require a lifetime of observation—providing opportunities for increasing our awareness of these fascinating creatures.

[1]F. Blanc, "Le cycle reproducteur chez la femelle de *Chamaeleo lateralis*," Gray, 1831. Ann. University, Madagascar, Sciences, 7, pp. 345–358: 1970.

[2]H. Saint Girons, "Présence de réceptacles séminaux chez la femelle *Chamaeleo lateralis*," Beaufortia 9 (106), pp. 165–172: 1963.

PART TWO

Chameleonids in Terrariums

Misunderstanding the behavior and the biology of chameleonids has led many reptile keepers to achieve mediocre results at best and at worst has resulted in ill or dead animals. No wonder so many hobbyists have been discouraged from further efforts to raise chameleons in captivity!

The chameleonid is a paradox. Contrary to what we may observe in an artificial environment, chameleonids drink sparingly in the wild. Much of the water needed by a wild chameleonid is absorbed from its humid surroundings as it breathes. Most chameleonids also prefer moderate to cool temperatures and are uncomfortable at the warm temperatures that other reptiles enjoy.

Part One of this book examined the biology and ecology of chameleonids. Part Two provides a practical guide to keeping and raising chameleonids. Bringing a chameleonid into your home means that you have decided to play nature's role. Before making this decision, you should read and understand the first part of this book. It is mandatory that you have sufficient resources to care properly for your pet. Many people wonder if it is possible to recreate an original biotope or habitat in the terrarium. I believe that, as long as top-quality materials are used and attention is paid to detail, it is possible to create terrariums that meet all the particular needs of each species.

Finally, your success will depend to a great extent on the health of the animals you receive. Whether you acquire your chameleonids from a breeder or through a pet store, purchase farm-raised animals, as opposed to wild-collected specimens. Call specialists if you are looking for a particular species, and do not hesitate to ask questions. Many breeders/hobbyists will be happy to explain details to you.

Important note: Two chameleon genera, *Chamaeleo* and *Bradypodion*, are protected by Appendix II of CITES (the Convention on International Trade of Endangered Species). Trade in these genera is legal but restricted, and varies by species and country. Be sure to check all of the applicable regulations before acquiring *Chamaeleo* or *Bradypodion* species.

Chamaeleo parsonii (male)

Chapter 7
The Ideal Terrarium

1. High-intensity discharge lamp
2. Wire mesh
3. Glass
4. Capillary matting
5. Substrate

Anyone who raises animals wants to encourage reproduction by creating favorable conditions. Therefore, it is necessary to set up the "ideal" terrarium for the species, an enclosure that goes as far as possible toward recreating the three main parameters of the habitat: temperature, humidity, and light.

The terrarium is divided into three parts: the area where the lighting, humidifier, and other equipment are kept (usually on the top of the tank);

A Typical Terrarium

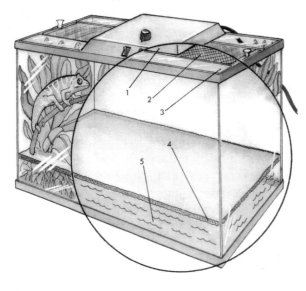

the viewing area/living quarters for the animals; and the substrate for the plants.

It is often better to have the terrarium specially built for your chameleonids. Some of your lizards may prefer to roam freely about a room in your home, returning to their "home" when tired of this exercise. Bear this in mind when building or buying your terrarium, and when placing it within your home.

Size

The size of the terrarium is based on the size of the animals being kept. Use L as the length of the largest chameleon and $2L$ for a pair of chameleons. Interior dimensions can be calculated on the basis of the size of the animal(s):
• Width = $2L$
• Length = $4L$
• Height = $3L$

Example: A pair of *Chamaeleo jacksonii* each 9 inches (22.9 cm) long would need a terrarium 36 inches (91.4 cm) wide, 72 inches (182.9 cm) long, and 54 inches (137.2 cm) high, with plenty of

branches to allow the animals access to all parts of their cage.

Light

Artificial lighting in a terrarium for chameleonids can be achieved with two types of light sources:
- high-intensity discharge lamps (HIDL, also known as actinic or metallic iodide lamps)
- fluorescent bulbs

High-intensity discharge lamps work the same way as fluorescent bulbs: a low-pressure gas is ionized and agitated by an electric current passing through it. The gas is composed of iodine and metalloids. The resulting light is rich in blue and violet rays, very similar to natural light. Because HIDL bulbs emit too many ultraviolet rays, a framework with a glass window is provided with the bulb to block these rays. In no case should this window be removed while the lamp is in use.

HIDL bulbs are among the most stimulating light sources currently available. Furthermore, it is possible to get flowers to blossom in a terrarium with HIDL.

Fluorescent bulbs give light that is inferior in quality and quantity to

A terrarium with high-intensity discharge lighting.

that produced by high-intensity discharge lamps. If you must use fluorescent bulbs, I recommend the full-spectrum daylight type.

Lighting and Enclosure Dimensions

One 250-watt actinic lamp (5,500° Kelvin) will illuminate 3.4 square feet (.32 m²) of surface up to a height of 20 inches (0.5 m). For the same dimensions, two full-spectrum fluorescent tubes will provide adequate lighting.

Type of Lighting According to Species

Shade-loving chameleonids—the stump-tails—will do sufficiently well in full-spectrum fluorescent lighting. However, because the majority of chameleonids are sun-loving, the only ideal lighting type is high-intensity discharge lamps.

Simultaneous use of full-spectrum fluorescent and high-intensity discharge lighting is possible in large terrariums.

Chamaeleo minor in a terrarium with flowering plants.

Intensity and Photoperiod

Ideally, lighting should reproduce natural lighting effects in quality and day length. For chameleonids, 12 to 14 hours of light a day is an average photoperiod. You can use actinic lamps exclusively or start off with fluorescents for three hours and turn on the HIDL when the temperature rises noticeably.

Heating

In their natural habitat chameleonids absorb heat by exposing themselves to the sun. They can do the same with high-intensity discharge lamps. These lamps give off sufficient light and heat to create a thermal gradient, thus allowing the animals to attain their preferred body temperature.

Note: All installations involving reptiles need to include certain areas with more cover.

Depending on local conditions, the heat of the ballast may be adequate for small terrariums illuminated with fluorescent lighting.

Humidity

A small water-circulating pump can raise the relative humidity in a small installation considerably. However, if your terrarium permits, I recommend an ultrasound humidifier. This apparatus is an excellent means of scattering "fog" in mountainous-type terrariums.

Plants in the Terrarium and the Substrate

Plants and substrates also play a part in regulating the humidity in the terrarium. The plants furnish cover for the animals and are certainly pleasing to the eye as well. Terrarium plants flourish in actinic lighting.

Branches should be provided so that the animals have ample place to exercise. For naturalistic terrariums, a layer of soil can be used to support shade-loving plants, although far better results can be obtained by incorporating new technologies. My most attractive terrariums have profited both from hydroponics and from actinic lighting. I have even been able to grow flowers from seeds I have sown.

The technique is simple. Just line the bottom of the terrarium with a suitable hydroponic substrate, cover with water, and add a capillary matting upon which the seeds are sown. Light helps the seeds germinate, and they will grow into very nice plants. The system is simple, neat, and good-looking.

Ventilation

The "new technology" terrariums afford adequate air circulation while maintaining an excellent level of humidity. For esthetic reasons, I provide ventilation apertures on the very top of my enclosures. I use a plastic mesh to cover half of the lid surface. Choose mesh with larger or smaller holes, depending on the species you are raising.

Equipment

Some equipment, such as a hygrometer, a thermometer, and an electric timer can be very useful in controlling the parameters of the environment in your terrarium.

There are now electronic digital thermometers with two sensors, one of which can be put at the hottest point of the terrarium, the other at the coolest point. In this way the temperature in the enclosure can be carefully controlled and, when necessary, adjusted to the chameleon's liking.

The hygrometer should be put in the most humid part of the setting (usually within the plantings); it will help you regulate the moisture in the air according to the species' need.

An electric timer can be useful if you wish to automate the environmental controls of your terrarium. The fog system can be set to go early in the morning; then the fluorescent lighting for about three hours; and then the actinic lamp, which provides light and heat.

Special Cautions

Year after year I have seen a parade of vague and misleading ideas on caring for chameleonids in a terrarium. Often these ideas are actually contrary to the animals' interests and result in failures by beginners. Therefore, I would like to offer the following suggestions.

Ultraviolet Ray Lamps

Ultraviolet (UV) rays are high-energy waves. In their presence the precursor of vitamin D is trans-formed into vitamin D_3. However, it was recently established that this photochemical process does not occur in chameleonids.[1]

While there are now safer UV lamps on the market, I believe that the use of ultraviolet ray lamps in the terrarium is potentially disastrous. The rays severely damage the plants and harm the animals, causing retinal disorders as well as second- and third-degree burns.

Heating

Heating wires (coils or strips) are a common feature in the terrarium. However, they are no asset in chameleonid maintenance. These wires tend to create a uniform temperature throughout the terrarium, but they can also burn the roots of the plants and the chameleonids as well. These lizards prefer solar rays/light as a source of heat.

Synthetic Plants and Soil

Use plastic plants and soil only if you're using plastic chameleonids. Real animals need real plants that take root in the earth and grow. Real plants absorb carbon dioxide, release oxygen, shelter and feed numerous insects, provide a stable temperature area, and regulate the humidity of the terrarium.

Drinking Water in Bowls

Chameleonids usually are unwilling to drink out of a bowl. Moreover, they could fall into the bowl of water and drown.

If you must put a little basin in your terrarium as a water source for other animals, be sure to put some branches across the container to give the chameleonid something to grasp should it fall into the water. The addition of an aquarium air stone, which will roil the water, might induce your chameleonids to drink.

Dry terrariums

Dry, or xeric, terrariums are not suited to chameleonids. If the air is too dry, the lizards will be affected physically. The mucous membranes and the eyes will dry out, adding vastly to the animals' discomfort, and waste excretion will be slowed, if not stopped.

Ventilation

Ventilation is necessary to avoid extremely hot temperatures, but if the terrarium is over-ventilated it is almost impossible to obtain ideal humidity and temperature. Ventilation is fine, but make sure it is well regulated.

How Many Chameleonids Can I Keep in a Terrarium?

This depends on a number of factors. First, how sociable is the species? Second, what are the comparative sizes and ages of the animals? The answer also depends on the size of the terrarium (see page 80), the amount of food available for each lizard, and the number of tree branches in the terrarium. Basically, each chameleonid should live in the most comfortable surroundings possible. Males of aggressive species should be housed separately or only with females.

[1]F. W. Henkel and S. Heinecke. *Chamaeleons im Terrarium. Landbuch*: 1994.

Chapter 8

The Different Types of Terrariums

Chameleon terrariums can be classified into six categories. The Sudanese, Sudano-Guinean, and forest-edge types are "hot" terrariums, meaning that *some* areas can reach 92°F (33.3°C). The forest terrarium is a transitional form between the hot and the "cool" terrariums. The cool terrariums are the plateau and the mountainous types, where the temperature must not exceed 82°F (28°C).

Sudanese

Temperature: 74 to 88°F (24–32°C).
Hygrometry: 60 to 70 percent.

Few chameleonids live in dry areas, so this kind of terrarium is intended for tropical sun-loving (heliophilous) species such as *C. chamaeleon, C. calyptratus*, and *C. namaquensis*.

Lighting and heating: The terrarium should be lit and heated with high-intensity discharge lamps. Expect to use one lamp for each 5.5 square feet (.5 m^2) placed 2 feet (.6 m) from the bottom of the terrarium.

Humidity: Humidify in the evening and early morning, using an artificial humidifier or misting device.

Substrate: The substrate should be composed of two layers of soil. Sand can be mixed with heath/peat to create the nutritive layer, with a layer of sand on top as a decorative stratum.

Chamaeleo chamaeleon (male) in a Sudanese terrarium.

Plants and decor: Choose plants that like heat and light (lemon tree, bougainvillaea, *Astrophytum, Stapelia, Myrtillocactus*). Be sure that the plants can supply sufficient cover for the animals.

Sudano-Guinean

Temperature: 74 to 84.2°F (24–29°C).
Hygrometry: 75 to 80 percent.
This type of terrarium is appropriate for *C. senegalensis, C africanus*, or *C. dilepis*—the species found in continental Africa—and for Madagascan species such as *C. oustaleti, C. lateralis major,* and *C. antimena.* Flowering plants (purslane, portulaca) or thick-leaved succulent (pachypodium, euphorbia) will thrive in light from actinic lamps. This is a hot and semi-humid terrarium.

Lighting and heating: The terrarium must be lit and heated with actinic lamps. Expect to use one lamp per 5.5 square feet (.5 m^2) placed 2 feet (.6 m) from the bottom of the terrarium.
Humidity: Humidify with an artificial humidifier or a small fountain in the terrarium.
Substrate: The substrate should be made of compost, vegetative matter in the process of decomposition. The bottom should be planted with grass or creepers.
Plants and decor: Bougainvillaea, *Ficus* sp. (or those listed above), dead branches.

Chamaeleo oustaleti in a Sudano-Guinean terrarium.

Forest Edge

Temperature: 73.5 to 86°F (23–30°C).
Hygrometry: 85–90 percent.
The species *C. gracilis, C. owenii, C. labordi,* and *C. pardalis* enjoy this type of habitat, a transi-

Chamaeleo labordi in a forest edge terrarium.

tion between the Sudano-Guinean and the forest types. It is a hot and humid terrarium.

Lighting and heating: The terrarium must be lit and heated with actinic lamps. Use one lamp for each 5 square feet (.45 m²), placed 20 inches (.5 m) from the bottom of the terrarium.

Humidity: Humidify with a basin, plants, and—in the evening—an artificial humidifier. The humidity may rise considerably during certain times of year.

Substrate: The substrate should be composed of two layers of soil. Use mix of sand, compost, heath/peat, and loam for the nutritive layer. You may also add a layer of dead leaves, bark, and moss.

Plants and decor: *Ficus, Dracaena, Polyscicus, Hibiscus, Syngonium, Heptaleurum, Caladium,* liana (creeper), climbing plants, and dead branches are suitable. A variety of insects (crickets, fruit flies) may be put into the terrarium to reproduce.

Chamaeleo gastrotaenia in a forest terrarium.

Forest

Temperature: 64.5 to 72.2°F (18–24°C).

Hygrometry: 90–100 percent.

This is one of the most interesting terrariums to create. The animals love this habitat if it is successfully simulated. This is the proper terrarium for the stump-tailed species. Some chameleonids will reproduce if the original seasons are followed.

It is possible to include numerous invertebrate species (fruit flies, blowflies, ants, termites) that can live on the organic waste produced in the terrarium.

Lighting and heating: Choose whatever heat source you prefer. Fluorescent lights or actinic lamps are both possible, providing the largest plants offer shade. For shade-loving chameleonids (*C. cucullatus, C. gastrotaenia,* and the various stump-tailed species) you will need fluorescent bulbs at the top of the tank. The bulbs should be as long as the terrarium, and there should be 6 inches (15 cm) of space between the bulbs.

Humidity: Humidify with a basin, plants, and—in the evening—an artificial humidifier.

Substrate: The substrate should be composed of two layers of soil. You may mix sand, heath/peat, and loam to create the nutritive layer. You may also cover it with a layer of dead leaves, bark, and moss.

Plants and decor: Use shade-loving plants such as *Begonia, Ficus, Fatsia, Cyrtonium, Phyllilus,*

Hedera, ferns, and lichen, epiphytes, dead branches, and lianas (creeper or vines).

Plateau

Temperature: 66 to 82°F (19–28°C).
Hygrometry: 75 to 90 percent.

This type of terrarium suits many chameleonids, even species originally from dry regions.

Don't confuse the habitat "plateau savanna," where *C. lateralis* and *C. minor* are found, with "plateau forest," a moister environment suitable for *C. p. parsoni, C. brevicornis,* and *C. w. willsii.*

Lighting and heating: The terrarium must be lit with high-intensity discharge (actinic) lamps. Expect to use one lamp for each 5 square feet (.45 m²), placed 20 inches (.5 m) from the bottom.

Humidity: Humidify with a mechanical humidifier.

Substrate: The substrate should be composed of one-third compost and two-thirds heath/peat for a plateau savanna. For the plateau forest type, the composition is identical to that for forest terrariums.

Plants and decor: You can use vegetation such as grasses and sedgelike plants. Garnish with dead branches or small shrubs. For chameleonids originally from a forested region, you must leave one-third of the terrarium open for more exposure to the actinic lamps, while leaving the other two-thirds shadier and much more humid. Provide a great many branches to help the animals move around to different areas.

Mountain

Temperature: 61 to 80°F (16–26.5°C).

Hygrometry: 85 to 100 percent.

This type of terrarium is particularly suited to species from higher elevations, such as *C. bitaeniatus, C. campani, C. demerensis, C. hohnelii, C. jacksonii, C. johnstoni, C. montium, C. quadricornus,* and *C. werneri*. If well done, it can have a remarkable effect.

Lighting and heating: The tank may be lit by fluorescent tubes (full-spectrum) and heated with an actinic lamp. You will need three fluorescent tubes for each 5 square feet (.45 m^2), placed 20 inches (.5 m) from the bottom of the terrarium. The actinic lamp (150 watts is sufficient) may be added in one area to create a "hot" spot.

Humidity: Humidify with a mechanical humidifier so as to maintain a very high humidity level.

Substrate: The substrate should be composed of a single layer of acidic soil for savanna habitats; for forest and mountain habitats, the forest terrarium substrate is a good choice.

Plants and decor: You may carpet the soil with varieties of vegetation: flowering plants, epiphytes, ferns, orchids, moss, and lichens.

Chamaeleon quadricornis juvenile in a mountain terrarium.

Greenhouses and Outdoor Enclosures

In certain climates, chameleonids can be kept in greenhouses or in outside enclosures for a part or even all of the year.

When well maintained, greenhouses and outdoor enclosures provide excellent habitats, but they are by no means superior to good terrariums.

Greenhouses

Greenhouses can be a practical place to keep large chameleonids, as these enclosures generally offer enough room for the animals to be happy. Babies should be kept in a smaller space where the temperature can be controlled.

Outdoor Enclosures

If climatic conditions correspond to those of the original habitat, one can observe the animals' behavior outdoors. The enclosures could contain dead leaves as well as living plants. Make sure the chameleonids are protected from other animals.

A greenhouse with a variety of tropical plants.

Chapter 9
Nutrition

Feed insects before you feed them to your chameleonids! The better-fed the insects, the better-fed your animals, and their appearance will reflect this.

The main ingredients of insect food are
- honey (sugar, trace elements, minerals, protein, vitamins, enzymes)
- pollen (protein, trace elements, minerals, fats, fiber)
- powdered milk (protein, sugar, fats, minerals: calcium, magnesium)
- amino acid complexes (protein)
- fish (protein, fats and oils, minerals: iodine, phosphorus, calcium)
- scrambled eggs (protein, fat, sugar, minerals)
- powdered algae or cabbage (minerals: calcium and iodine)
- vitamin complex
- rehydration salts (minerals)

Nourishment in Accordance with Needs

The chameleonids' food must provide them with all the energy they need. The food ration is sufficient if

- it supplies the elements needed to produce energy;
- it supplies good-quality protein and related materials to ensure growth and physical health;
- it contains sufficient quantities of minerals (sodium, potassium, magnesium, calcium) and trace elements (iron, copper, manganese, zinc, sulfur, iodine, selenium);
- it is vitamin-rich;
- it provides a healthy balance between bulk and nutritional value;
- it is not toxic.

Pay special attention to the following requirements:

Maintenance Needs
These needs are defined as the quantity of nourishment that the animal must have each day to maintain a constant weight and to remain in good health. They do not take into consideration the extra nutrition needed for reproduction. To ensure the right dose for maintenance needs, feed your insects one-third of the reproduction-needs dose.

Reproduction Needs
These needs represent the quantity of nourishment above and

This female *Chamaeleo willsii willsii* died of suffocation. Eggs can be seen up to her throat.

beyond the maintenance rations that an animal requires to produce eggs (or to accomplish other special functions) without having to tap its reserves. Obviously the nutritional requirements also increase during gestation.

Enhancing the formula fed to insects can provide the necessary nutritive boost. Here is the "magic potion" you should feed to the insects (flies and crickets), by percentage of the total volume:

- water   30
- honey   20
- scrambled eggs 15
- pollen   10
- amino acids   10
- rehydration salts 10
- vitamin complex 5

Alternatively, you could use one of the commercial insect rations that are now available in pet stores.

Egg formation in the female's body consumes a great deal of energy and a great many food elements. As the eggs grow, they become heavier and take up more and more room in the body cavity (sometimes as much as 50 percent of the female's weight and up to 80 percent of the body cavity). Food bulk in relation to its nutritive value has to be reduced. Since chameleons readily accept flies, the volume reduction/nutrient enhancement can be accomplished by giving the female chameleons a diet of flies that have fed only on the reproduction-needs formula.

Growth Needs

Growth needs are defined as the quantity of food required by both the young and the adult chameleonids, beyond the maintenance ration. The growth diet allows the lizards not only to construct their bones, muscles, and internal organs, but also to build up

63

reserves. The net result is daily weight gain.

Reptiles continue to grow throughout their lives. It is therefore essential to take into account growth and reproduction needs when feeding chameleonids in a terrarium.

Many guides for terrarium hobbyists state that chameleonids need daily exposure to ultraviolet rays to synthesize their vitamin D. Vitamin D enhances gut absorption of calcium through the production of calcium-binding protein (CaBP). Calcium is necessary for homeostasis of the blood, bone construction, contraction of skeletal and cardiac muscle, blood clotting, etc.

The statement regarding the UV requirements of chameleonids is based on their sensitivity to the quality and intensity of light, which influences both their activity and their biological cycles. Moreover, most of these lizards are sun-loving species that bask in the morning sunlight to warm up.

The provitamins and vitamin D are widely but weakly disseminated. They are found in notable quantities in animal livers and skin, as well as in some vegetable oils. Generally animals obtain their vitamin D from two sources: by photosynthesis from phenols in particular parts of their skin that are sensitive to specific UV rays; or from the foods they ingest.

French scientist M. Deribere took photos of *Chamaeleo chamaeleon* with Kodak Atimax 3200ISQ film and an 18A filter, thereby exposing the film only to ultraviolet rays. These photos demonstrated that the skin of the subjects *reflected* the UV rays instead of absorbing them.[1] Therefore, it is probable that chameleons get their vitamin D from food rather than from UV exposure. (See also page 54 and footnote.)

Nutritional Illnesses

What effect do gastric, renal, starvation, and hepatic (biliary) problems have on the health of the animals? Such problems can result in acid or alkaline autointoxication of the metabolic system. This topic will be discussed in the remainder of this chapter.

Protein Deficiencies

A chameleonid in the wild moves around in search of food. It keeps moving until it finds food or until it dies. A captive chameleonid cannot journey until it finds food; food must be supplied. If the right food is not supplied in the right quantities, the animal will develop protein deficiencies and waste away.

Vitamin Deficiencies and Excess

A lack or an excess of vitamins will prevent the assimilation of mineral salts, which will then be present in too large a quantity in the blood and the urine. According to Finlayson and Woods, vitamin D given in excess—either (d_2) or 1.25

dihydroxycholecalciferol—will lead to poor bone formation. They suggest an adequate dose to be 100 i.u. (international units)/kg/week.

The growth problems that some breeders encounter in their breeding programs are more often due to a lack of iodine in the food than to vitamin imbalance. For example, vitamin A toxicity in chameleonids has recently been studied and described, but although high levels of vitamin A in the chameleon's food "led to edema in the neck and throat area and, in the advanced stages, to anemia and bone decalcification,"[2] correcting the vitamin A balance in the diet was not enough to get rid of the phenomenon. The restoration of iodine was also necessary.

Mineral Deficiencies

Mineral deficiencies can lead to poor bone formation. A bad diet is usually the cause, the food being low in calcium and iodine. Lack of proper nutrition, like rickets, can cause the animals to be dwarfed. Calcium can be supplied to the food insects via pulverized cuttlebone or powdered milk. Large quantities of iodine are found in dried algae and cabbage. Administering vitamins and minerals by "packing" the food insects does not put the animal's health at risk.

Chameleonids lose water through their skin (see page 22), but this loss is largely passive. It depends not on physiological control, but on skin permeability and ambient humidity. Most salts are secreted through the nasal glands.

For these reasons, it is important to maintain the correct humidity in the tank and to make sure the diet is properly balanced in salts. To prevent problems it is best to feed the food insects with honey, pollen, powdered milk, and occasional pieces of fish. A diet deficient in iodine may result in loss of appetite.

Iodine is also important for proper growth. It can be administered as a dietary supplement, or as a weekly treatment with a dosage of 1 mg of potassium iodide for each gram of body weight.

Healthy animals need only a moderate amount of mineral salts in their food.

Acidosis and Alkalosis

Chameleonids sometimes suffer from electrolyte imbalance, due to stresses such as illness, starvation, or elevated temperature. If the bicarbonate concentration is above normal, the condition is called alkalosis; if it is below normal, acidosis results. It is important to know how to diagnose these conditions, especially when you purchase a chameleon, and how to treat them.

Each condition has two forms:
- Metabolic acidosis: typified by increased production of acids stronger than H_2CO_3 (carbonic acid) and/or diarrhea. This form of acidosis may be triggered by starvation, violent, stressful physical efforts, or acid retention following kidney malfunction.

Chamaeleo parsonii (yellow lip type). This may be a new subspecies.

• Respiratory acidosis: typified by diminished expiration of CO_2, resulting in an increase in the amount of carbonic acid in the blood.

• Metabolic alkalosis: typified by loss of acids due to vomiting or following the administration of alkalizing salts. It may be triggered by sodium bicarbonate or sodium lactate.

• Respiratory alkalosis: typified by rapid respiration. This form of alkalosis may be triggered by intense heat.

The animal can be restored to normal through oral administration of salt solutions in distilled water or glucose for two days.

For acidosis, use sodium lactate solution at 1.75 percent in 5 percent glucose water. For alkalosis, use ammonium chloride at 0.8 percent in an isotonic solution. In the case of respiratory alkalosis, add a small amount of potassium chloride.

Oral administration can be performed with a round-tipped catheter tube, which you can slip into the animal's esophagus while tilting the head upwards.

Only one treatment is advisable, owing to the animal's weakened physiological state. An overdose of liquid must be avoided.

To sum up: surpluses or deficiencies of food, mineral salts, or protein can damage your animal's health. A balanced selection of foods served frequently and in moderate amounts is the best bet for healthy growth.

[1] M. Deribere, "*Le caméléon: un caprice de la nature.*" EREC. Ed: 1980.
[2] J. M. Annis, "Hypervitaminosis A in Chameleons," *Chameleon Information Network* #9:[nd].

Chapter 10
Raising Insects

Should I Raise My Own Insects?

Raising insects—except *drosophila* (fruit flies)—may not justify the time and trouble it entails. Suppliers can usually provide you with live food all year, but the decision is yours.

Migrating Locusts

Locusta migratoria, Schistocerca gregaria

Although migrating locusts are not available in the United States, they can be purchased readily in many other countries.

Where Can I Buy the Stock?
- from private breeders (read the classified ads in entomological and terrarium newsletters and magazines)
- from entomological clubs
- from local universities and natural history museums

Raising Locusts

Although raising locusts is easy, it is inconvenient because of the odors generated. The eggs of some species must go through a one- to three-month cooling period. During cooling the eggs undergo a diapause (cessation of development) critical to hatching success. The breeders of the stock in question should be able to provide additional details.

Locusts reproduce easily and the young grow rapidly. The young of *L. migratoria* are orange and black; those of *S. gregaria* are yellowish-pink and black. Both may be fed grassy corn sprouts and oat flakes. Locusts are excellent food for chameleons. They are rich in calcium and vitamin D, which they obtain from the corn sprouts and oat flakes on which they feed. *S. Gregaria,* however, are preferable because they also feed eagerly on cabbage, which is an excellent source of vitamin C, calcium, magnesium, and iodine.

Locusts lay their eggs (ootheca) in humid sand. For this reason, reproducing adults need pots of sand in which the females can lay their eggs—generally 30 to 50 per clutch. The eggs have to be transferred to another cage and incubated at 90°F (32°C). Eggs that do not require a diapause take two to three weeks to hatch. Upon hatching the young should be placed in a screen cage (use metal, not plastic screening). All will soon shed their "skins." The hatchlings should be fed finely minced wheat germ and flakes of bran daily. A piece of water-saturated cotton in a shallow dish should also be provided to satisfy the baby locusts' moisture requirements. The young undergo five successive sheddings before attaining adult size ("L5"). The intermediate stages ("L2" through "L4") may be used for food. Adults begin reproduction one week after the last shedding. Adult females are larger than the males and become sterile after one month.

A mortality rate of 10 to 15 percent is normal during the growth period.

To sprout wheat (from which bran is derived):

1. Buy non-treated wheat from health food stores.
2. Soak the wheat in water for three days.
3. Sow the thoroughly soaked wheat in a trough containing coarse vermiculite and keep in a well-lit place.
4. Replant a new crop daily.

Why Locusts?

Locusts are grass-eating insects and the main source of calcium for most chameleons in the wild. Captive chameleons may be fed cheaper insects and given locusts from time to time as a special treat.

Crickets

Acheta domestica, Gryllus bimaculatus, G. campestris

Where Can I Buy the Stock?

- from private and commercial breeders, fishing and pet shops
- from entomological and terrarium clubs
- from universities and natural history museums

Raising Crickets

Raising crickets is particularly easy. Unfortunately, it can also be quite smelly.

Although crickets are best raised separately, those placed in terrariums as food insects often breed if conditions are suitable. The requirements are warmth, food, water, and soil in which to lay their eggs. Since crickets are cannibalistic, it is advisable to separate the eggs and young from the adults, ideally by offering the adults a separate egg-deposition container. Merely move the "full" egg container to another terrarium with a suitable temperature. There the young can hatch and grow.

Crickets eagerly feed on pollen. Do not hesitate to supply this very rich food to your insects before you give them to your chameleons.

Why Crickets?

Crickets are among the most readily available and inexpensive food insects. They will eat a wide variety of foods, including fish, carrots, oranges, dog food, and broccoli. By "gut-loading" the crickets with such items before feeding them to your lizards, the chameleons will get the advantage of the vitamins and minerals in the crickets' last meal. Pollen (available from health food stores) is an excellent food eagerly accepted by crickets.

Flies

Musca domestica

How Can I Obtain the Stock?
- by trapping flies yourself
- by buying maggots in fishing and pet shops

Raising Flies
I trap flies with a tilted bell jar under which I put a little water and a piece of fish. The results are extraordinary during hot weather. A second way to get flies is to raise them yourself by pupating the maggots available from various sources. Keep the maggots in a well ventilated place at about 90°F(32°C). As pupae prepare to metamorphose into adult flies, they become very dark in color. At that point, to retard emergence, they can be kept in a refrigerator. Remove a few of the pupae as you need them, keeping them in a tightly covered container and allowing them to reach room temperature. The flies will emerge a few hours later. It is best to feed the flies heavily before offering them to your chameleons. Prepare a paste of equal proportions of a good multivitamin supplement, pollen, pulverized cuttlefish bone, powdered milk, honey, and rehydration salts. The flies will relish this healthy mix.

Why Flies?
Many chameleons, after becoming bored with crickets, readily accept flies. Moreover, maggots are inexpensive, easily metamorphosed, and, if gut-loaded, very nutritious.

Wax Worms

Galleria mellanela

Where Can I Buy the Stock?
- from beekeepers
- from bait and pet shops

Raising Wax Worms
I don't advise raising wax worm caterpillars unless you wish to have them all over your house! It is best to schedule regular pickups from a breeder or beekeeper. You can raise wax worms on a paste made of
- 6 ounces (175 g) honey
- 2.7 ounces (75 g) powdered wheat germ
- 6 ounces (175 g) glycerine
- 3.7 ounces (75 g) yeast
- 17.6 ounces (500 g) corn flowers
- 17.6 ounces (500 g) pollen

The ingredients are usually available from health food stores.

Put the paste in a metal box with a lid perforated for ventilation and keep it at a temperature range of 77 to 84.4°F (25–29°C) and a relative humidity of 30 percent. Place several pairs of moths in the box. The females will quickly lay their eggs on the bread. The larvae will hatch in 14 days and consume the paste. Metamorphosis is complete in about 40 days. To slow the growth of wax worm caterpillars, keep them at 50°F (10°C).

Why Wax Worms?

These highly nutritious insects, which contain about 70 percent protein, plus fat, provide chameleons with an excellent and much-appreciated "energy food."

Mealworms

Tenebrio molitor, Zoophobas sp.

Where Can I Buy the Stock?
• from pet and bait shops
• from commercial breeders

Raising Mealworms

These worms are easily raised in a terrarium or in a tub containing bran mixed with powdered wheat-germ, brewer's yeast, pieces of carrot, and chopped fruit.

Why Mealworms?

Large chameleons readily accept the larger species of mealworm, *Zoophobas* sp. Much speculation exists as to the actual food value of the smaller species, *Tenebrio molitor*. *Zoophobas* seems to be more nutritious and less fattening than *Tenebrio*. Neither should be used as an exclusive food item.

Fruit Flies

Drosophila funebrus, D. melanoleuca

How Can I Obtain the Stock?
• by trapping fruit flies
• from commercial breeders
• from biological supply houses
• from university biology departments, laboratories, natural history museums

Raising Fruit Flies

True to their name, fruit flies are quickly attracted to fermenting fruit. They are easily raised, requiring only a few small, covered glass jars and food. To feed them, make a paste of two rusks (crackers or toast), a mashed banana, two cups of yogurt, two tablespoons of multivitamin dietary supplement, a teaspoon of Nipagine (or any other bacteriostat).

The fruit flies will breed prolifically if kept at 86°F (30°C). Once established, each colony will produce 10 or more fruit flies daily. Use the jars in rotation.

Why Fruit Flies?

They are ideal food insects for both hatchling chameleons and the adults of the smallest species (e.g., *C. asuta, Brookesia* sp.).

Plant Lice

Myzus persicae, Aphis sp.

How Can I Obtain the Stock?
• Plant lice (aphids) are common warm-weather plant pests in gardens, orchards, groves, and greenhouses. Be sure not to gather them where insecticides have been used.

- They may also occasionally be available from biology labs.

Raising Plant Lice

Plant lice are not easy to breed, but once established they are prolific. They are also common in the wild. Once you have found an insecticide-free wild colony, you should be able to draw on it for some time. The peach-tree aphid, *Myzus persicae*, is one of the easiest species to propagate. The tubs or trays in which they are kept must be tightly covered with fine wire or mesh netting to prevent the winged adults from escaping. These aphids become especially restless when crowded. They need 12 to 13 hours of daylight daily and a temperature of 71 to 74°F (20–23.5°C). Freshly cut or growing stems of nourishing green plants (*not* the fruits) such as tomatoes, beans, peas, or eggplants must always be kept available as feed.

The lice can be collected by running fine tweezers along the plant stems.

Why Plant Lice?

Aphids are a natural and healthy food for all small chameleon species as well as for the hatchlings of larger species.

Chapter 11

Inducing Reproduction in Captive Chameleonids

Chameleonids reproduce easily in the terrarium if conditions are favorable. The recreation of the climatic conditions of the chameleon's natural habitat is essential, because it is they that trigger sexual activity.

In the wild, reproductive functions peak shortly after periods of dormancy. Alternatively, they may be triggered by a change in rainfall or photoperiod. For certain species (*C. p. parsonii*), reproduction can occur only after a cool rest period.

Hibernation and Aestivation

Rest periods, even short ones, are indispensable for most chameleonids. The period of winter (or cooler season) dormancy is termed hibernation. A summer (or warmer season) period of dormancy is termed aestivation.

It is possible to induce hibernation or aestivation in captive chameleons. Note that some species hibernate or aestivate in the ground, while others remain quietly on tree branches to await moderating temperatures.

Important note: It is mandatory that your chameleonids fast for several days before you induce hibernation or aestivation. Digestive processes slow or stop when your chameleon is dormant. If its stomach and intestines are not food-free, gut contents can putrefy. This can be fatal to your lizard.

When inducing either hibernation or aestivation (except in the case of montane chameleon species), you must lower humidity and decrease soil moisture until surface drying is seen.

Hibernation/Aestivation of True Chameleons

Chameleons can be compared to batteries. If you use them at 100 percent of their capacities all the time, they won't last long. It is best to alternate very active periods with periods of dormancy. After at least three days of fasting, temperature should be gradually lowered and the animals allowed to rest. The decrease in temperature, light, and humidity will make the chameleons sleepy. Provide branches and main-

Chamaeleo rhinoceratus hibernating.

tain these climatic parameters: 57 to 68°F (14-20°C), 60 percent humidity. Keep the terrarium well shaded. Hibernating chameleons will benefit from a two- to three-week break under these conditions every year. Some species require somewhat longer periods of decreased activity. Water should be offered at least once a week. Shorter rest periods (one or two days) should also be offered to chameleons about once a month.

Certain species (*C. chameleon, C. campani, C. höhnelii, C. j. jacksonii, C. bitaeniatus, C. eliotti, Bradypodion* sp.), but no pregnant ovoviviparous females should remain out-side during moderately adverse climatic conditions.

Aestivation occurs in some cases with equatorial and tropical species. The chameleons are dormant, but they still need food and water to survive. Rations should be offered at the beginning or end of the day. Because of the adverse conditions, aestivating chameleons spare their energy during the remaining daylight hours by taking shelter in the foliage of trees.

Hibernation and Aestivation of Stump-tailed Chameleons

During cool, inclement weather, all stump-tailed chameleons take refuge

Brookesia legenderi.

in burrows in the soil. Therefore, you must provide these species with soil sufficiently deep for burrowing. You may wish to make, or at least start, little burrows for the lizards in the soil. A layer of dead leaves atop the soil may be beneficial.

Species that aestivate live in both humid equatorial and primary tropophile (deciduous) forests. A slight increase in temperature—3.5 to 5.5°F (2-3°C)—and a drop in humidity trigger aestivation.

Although the length of these rest periods may vary from one to several weeks, the periods of absolute rest are generally fairly short and occur only during the periods of coldest (hibernation) or hottest (aestivation) weather.

To trigger aestivation in the stump-tail terrarium, the humidity must decrease to the point at which the grass becomes dry. An average humidity of 60 percent and a temperature of 79°F(26°C) are usually adequate. To a terrarium in which stump-tails are aestivating you might add colonies of termites, springtails, or other small insects from the forest floor. Then your stump-tails will always be able to find food during their periods of wakefulness. Sprinkle the terrarium every three weeks to humidify it. Stump-tailed chameleons can easily live in these conditions for two months.

To trigger hibernation in the stump-tail terrarium, lower the temperature to 58°F (14°C). It is important that the animals be fasting. For stump-tails, true hibernation must last from one to two months. During this period the animals eat nothing.

Reproduction

When breeding chameleonids, you may house them as a pair or place several females with one male. Keeping a single pair together is the more usual method. To prevent undue harassment of the female(s) by the male, separate the sexes once your chameleonids

Chamaeleo calyptratus (male and female) mating.

Egg Incubation Temperature (in degrees Fahrenheit)

Sector	Too Low	Ideal	Too High
Sudanese*	59	72–82.4	86
Sudano-Guinean*	62.6	72–79	85
Forest Edge*	65	73–78.5	83
Forest**	63.5	70–74	80.6
Plateau*	55	70–74	81
Mountain**	53.5	72–74	78

* Noted for lengthy incubation periods.
** No fluctuation in temperature and very little in humidity.

have bred. Some breeders prefer to house the sexes separately except for brief periods when the female is placed in the male's enclosure.

Female chameleonids are capable of storing viable sperm. This allows oviparous species to produce more than a single clutch of fertile eggs (or delaying fertilization and laying until climatic conditions are suitable for egg incubation) and ovoviviparous species to produce more than a single clutch of living young.

Females of certain species must make an enormous and exhausting effort to produce their eggs. To accomplish this they must maintain the best of health. Ample nourishment is especially important (see page 62). Oviparous species select their nesting site carefully. At the chosen site the earth will contain adequate (but not excessive) moisture and retain a suitably warm temperature. Often females choose the moistest spot in the terrarium for egg deposition. Other sites might be the summit or edge of a

soil mound, a spot near the root mass of a plant, or a barren area.

Egg Incubation

The substrate: Correct development of the embryos depends on retention of suitable soil moisture and maintenance of a constant temperature throughout the incubation term. In nature, eggs are laid in soil or leaves, both natural bacteriostatics. Although the eggs have their own immune system and are rarely subject to microbial problems, when they are incubated in captivity I prefer to use sphagnum moss, itself a bacteriocide. With a pH of 5.5 or less, the sphagnum does much to lessen the potential for problems.

Humidity and soil moisture content: In nature, a sharp increase in relative humidity and soil moisture during the final two weeks of incubation seems to stimulate embryo development and facilitate hatching. In captivity, one should strive to duplicate natural conditions. In the egg incubation temperature table, tropical chameleon species noted for their lengthy incubation are indicated with an asterisk. The long duration results from

1. the eggs' being laid at an early (though variable) stage of embryonic development
2. the fact that a diapause in development occurs during the dry season

The return of the rainy season restarts the development of the eggs. Air and substrate humidity in the incubator must remain between 85 and 100 percent.

Temperatures: As we have seen in the analysis of environmental factors, soil temperature directly affects the embryonic development of chameleon eggs. Cold temperatures retard development; warm temperatures accelerate development somewhat. It is now known that, like adult chameleonids, chameleonid eggs withstand cool temperatures better than high ones.

Questions and Answers about Chameleonid Eggs and Their Care

• *Can I move the eggs without risk?*

I have, on occasion, handled and moved fertile chameleonid eggs. All have hatched without problems. I am not yet ready to form a conclusion based on these experiments.

• *Is it true that the eggs take a long time to hatch?*

Yes. In the wild it can take 16 to 21 months for eggs to hatch (*C. parsonii*). The length of the incuba-

Chamaeleo nasutus (male), the smallest species of the chameleon genus.

tion period depends on temperature, soil moisture, and the stage of embryonic development at which the eggs were laid. The smaller the eggs are when laid in relation to the size of the adult and the greater the number of eggs, the longer it takes them to hatch.

- *Should I remove the eggs from the place where they were laid?*

I do. I place the eggs on a bed of sphagnum moss to provide an acidic and antibacterial environment, then cover them with another layer of sphagnum. I make sure the eggs remain in a moist environment at all times.

- *Should I worry about eggs that swell and break?*

Swelling is a good sign. If the eggs begin to shrink, however, the embryos cannot continue to develop. When the eggs crack and begin to ooze a bit of white, hatching time is near. Be patient and allow the babies to reabsorb the yolk. The baby breaks through the egg 24 to 48 hours after the initial cracking.

- *Is the egg still good if yellow-brown spots appear on the shell?*

As long as the egg remains firm and supple when touched and the shell isn't damaged, then the egg is good. However, if fungus, bumps, or holes appear, it should be removed from the clutch. An infection-retarding membrane envelops each egg. For this reason eggs should never be washed.

Caring for Young Chameleonids

Young chameleonids may be kept together but should be separated from the adults. Put the babies in a terrarium that is slightly cooler and more humid than the adults'. Feed the babies two or three times daily, systematically supplementing their food with vitamin and mineral additives. Flies usually are eagerly accepted by babies. Since flies can be bred or collected in large numbers and readily ingest liquid dietary supplements, they are a good food choice for young chameleonids.

Chapter 12
Health and Medical Aspects

How can one tell whether a chameleonid is in good health? By good health we mean both physical and psychological well-being. Physical well-being is guaranteed if the animal can find in its environment the elements necessary to maintain its organic functions. Psychological well-being is assured if proper care, protection, and relatively stress-free living conditions are provided by the keeper.

Captive-bred animals are always more satisfactory than wild-collected specimens. Lizards from the wild often arrive stressed, dehydrated, and heavily parasitized. It is difficult to overcome these problems, either singly or in combination. Veterinary procedures for reptiles are only now coming into their own, and medications and purges are still being developed. Captive-bred specimens may live nearly twice as long as wild-collected specimens.

How Can I Tell If My Chameleonid Is Healthy?

If you were going to buy a fish to cook for supper, you would carefully choose only a fresh one. Apply similar standards when you purchase a chameleonid. Healthy, attractive skin texture is important. Properly kept specimens have an alert appearance and their rounded turret-like eyes are not sunken. The interior of the mouth should be clean, well-lubricated and free of sores, injuries and discolorations.

A healthy male *Chamaeleo cucullatus.*

A sick female *Chamaeleo balteatus*.

How Can I Recognize a Sick Animal?

Any abnormal behavior such as prostration, loss of balance, and loss of appetite requires immediate clinical examination.

Does the Chameleonid Need Exercise?

Chameleonids (except the stump-tailed species) often like to get out of their terrarium and roam. However, they also like to return to the terrarium once they have finished their stroll. Exercise promotes their general well-being.

Prophylactic Measures

The best way to ward off disease while keeping and breeding chameleonids is to have only healthy specimens to begin with. After ascertaining that your lizards meet those requirements, avoid contact with the potentially infectious germ carriers (obviously sick or wild-collected specimens) and the main parasite carriers (biting insects, mollusks from streams and ponds, and small wild animals—in particular, those from tropical areas).

Sanitary precautions will help maintain the health of your captive-bred chameleonids; medical intervention will help restore them to health when accidents or illnesses occur.

Sanitary Considerations

Microbes and parasites do not appear spontaneously. To prevent and treat illness, it is vital to understand how pathogenic agents are transmitted.

Pathogens may be transmitted by contagion (virus, bacteria), ingestion (mycosis), stings and bites from invertebrates (insects or mites), or contact with infected or unclean surroundings or agents, such as feces, air, water, soil, or grass that may harbor protozoans, the eggs of endoparasites, or other harmful organisms.

Important note: Unhealthy chameleonids should be isolated from other specimens at all times. The method of treatment depends on the type of illness and the means of its transmission.

Asymptomatic illnesses also exist. Some chameleonids may exhibit no clinical signs of disease yet actually be carriers of one or more illnesses.

Examine your potential purchases carefully. Check the specimen's skin, nasal orifices, the edge of the mouth, and the cloacal openings. The skin should be clean and healthy, and there should be no discharge from the orifices. The eyes should not be sunken. There should be no encrustations on the eyelids. The joints should not be swollen.

If doubt as to the health of the specimen remains, have a veterinarian check a blood sample for filaria and protozoans and a fecal workup to test for other pathogens.

Medical Considerations

The importance of this topic cannot be overestimated. The material that follows is merely an introduction. Refer to more specialized works (see page 122) and consult your veterinarian for further information.

Once again, I must stress the importance of acquiring captive-bred specimens. Most of the health problems of chameleons are caused by parasites encountered in the wild. If you have no choice or have decided that you must have a particular import, deal only with responsible specialists.

Knowledge of reptile diseases and their treatments has increased dramatically within the last few years. Today there are many veterinarians who specialize in reptile medicine, and new treatments and procedures are being developed almost daily. It is now possible to obtain professional opinions and help on the subjects of reptile anesthesia and surgery as well as advice on prevention. Dedicated researchers continue to add to this store of knowledge, and the input shows no signs of lagging.

Antibiotics are a principal component of the arsenal of medications used to combat reptile diseases. The bacteria they combat are easily identified and very often a cause of organic disorders. However, one should not forget that many of the drugs and antibiotics are themselves toxic and, if administered incorrectly, may be fatal to the specimens. Since the metabolism of poikilotherms is not comparable to that of mammals, the evaluation of medication dosages in the past was most often empirical. This lack of knowledge meant that the reptiles suffered. Now, thanks to various veterinary colleges, a method exists for accurately calculating the preferred dosages of antibiotics for many species of reptiles. New and updated information is accruing at unprecedented rates.

Should your chameleonid experience a major health problem, take it immediately to a veterinarian qualified in the treatment of reptile diseases. Take this book along; its information could prove useful.

Infectious Diseases

Pathological agents can be classified according to size, from the smallest to the largest, as follows: viruses, bacteria, protozoans, fungi, and parasites.

A sick *Chamaeleo johnstoni* female.

It is normal for an animal to come into contact with numerous potential pathogens throughout its lifetime. The chance of the animal's becoming seriously ill from contact with microbes is heightened if its normal defenses are weakened by stress or injury.

Viruses

Viruses are elementary life-forms, visible only under the magnifications provided by electron microscopes. They are able to multiply only inside the living cells of their host. Their pathogenic action results from this multiplication. Viruses have not yet been identified in chameleons, but that does not mean that the possibility of their existing in chameleons should be ruled out. Since the virus dies when the host dies, viruses are impossible to identify post-mortem.

Bacteria

Bacteria are single-celled organisms without a nucleus. They multiply by fission and are classified according to shape:
- round *Staphylococcus, Streptococcus*
- curved *Vibrio*
- spiral *Spirochetes*
- straight *Bacillus*

The pathogenic action of bacteria is due to secreted toxins (*Clostridium* sp.) and infections caused by multiplication (*Salmonella* sp.).

Local Infections

Abscesses: Most subcutaneous abscesses are easily recognized:

They appear as well-defined pus-filled sacs just beneath the skin. On internal organs they are more difficult to find. Abscesses are often caused by gram-negative bacteria. These subcutaneous lesions must be surgically removed by a veterinarian, the resulting sores thoroughly cleansed, and the entire area kept clean and sterile through the use of Neomycin or Betadine solutions until healing is completed.

Dermatitis: Dermatitis appears first as an ulceration, which is followed by skin necrosis. When the skin degrades and cracks, lymph oozes through the openings. The area should be swabbed with Betadine two or three times a day. If the sores are gaping, the veterinarian will perform a sensitivity test to determine what bacteria are present and to what antibiotic they are susceptible. Daily subcutaneous injections with sterile saline containing 5 percent glucose will prevent dehydration and electrolyte loss. Dermatitis commonly afflicts *C. j. johnstoni*.

Cloacitis: Clinical signs are ulceration of cloacal tissues and cloacal swellings. The area will be very sensitive. Failure to expel a solid object (stone, etc.) may be the cause. After verification, the object must be surgically removed by a veterinarian and tests made for the presence of pathogens. Should pathogens be present, they must be eradicated.

Eye infections: Conjunctivitis is rare but possible in chameleons.

Secondary infection resulting from a poorly treated or untreated primary infection (nasal infection, stomatitis) is more common. The resulting abscess(es) should be carefully excised by a veterinary surgeon and the resulting lesions cleansed with a streptomycin solution. Continue the cleansing two or three times a day for the next five to six days (until healing is obvious).

Infectious stomatitis (mouth rot): Symptoms include complete loss of appetite, suspicious swelling and/or caseous matter or scabbing on the lips, and skin discoloration and sensitivity. The oral mucus will display white, cheese-like masses.

A number of bacteria could be responsible. Treat the swellings/sores daily with powdered tetracycline or with an antibiotic with a tetracycline base. Your veterinarian may prescribe intramuscular injections of tetracycline, which is administered at a dosage of 50 mg/ml/kg. The injections should be administered daily for five to seven days.

General Infections

Septicemia (blood poisoning): Septicemia is a blood infection caused by bacteria, for the most part gram-negative *Aeromonas* and *Pseudomonas*. Septicemias are difficult to spot, and their progress can be very rapid or very slow. Diagnosis is often at the post-mortem. These infections can occur at the same time as gastroenteritis (amoebic dysentery caused by

Entamoeba), when the amoebas cause ulcers in the intestinal mucus and allow pathogenic bacteria to enter the bloodstream, where they multiply. They may also appear with bacteria (*Shigella* spp., Salmonella spp.) or with a parasitic infection (helminthiasis of the digestive system).

Since septicemias are secondary infections, it is best to treat them by eliminating the primary infection first, under the direction of your veterinarian, who will then attack the septicemia—generally with an intramuscular injection of tetracycline, 60 mg/ml/kg once a day for five days.

Protozoans

In the wild, blood parasites of chameleonids include *Trypanosoma therezieni* and *Leishmania* spp.

Chamaeleo dilepsis.

These particular protozoans are transmitted by flies, while others (*Haemogregarina* spp.) are transmitted by ticks or mosquitoes. These parasites destroy the red blood cells, and anemia results. So far there is no known medical treatment.

I know of no amoebic illnesses occurring in chameleonids in the wild.

Fungus

Skin mycosis: When fungus develops on the skin, it damages the skin tissues and leads to further complications. (The role of bacteria and protozoans has not yet been defined.) When *Fusarium oxysporum* has affected chameleons such as *C. dilepsis* or *C. melleri*, the lesions should be swabbed with Betadine, along with a daily regimen of Daktar ointment applied locally and externally.

Respiratory mycosis: The most obvious symptom is breathing difficulty. Internally, nodules and lesions develop on the mucous tissues of the lungs. Your veterinarian may recommend treatment with Hydroxystilbamidin or Griseofulvin.

Digestive system mycosis: Granular lesions that tend to be generalized (*Paercilomyces* sp.; *Fularium folani* with *C. jacksonii*) lead to ulcers and necrosis of the intestine. In *C. chameleon*, the cloaca becomes necrotic.

There is no known medical treatment. Fortunately, digestive mycoses are rare in chameleons.

Chamaeleo bitaeniatus.

Organic mycosis: The lesions are due to the production of mycotoxins. Affected organs are the liver (*C. höhnelii* and *C. bitaeniatus*) and the areas around the joints (*C. pardalis, C. brevicornis, C. chamaeleon*). Certain specimens experience extreme swelling of the joints, due to a fungus of the *Aspergillus* type.

Pentastome

Also called linguatids, pentastomes are pararthropods—a group related to the arthropods (mites, ticks). They are found in most of the tropical lizards and also in birds, snakes, mammals, and other animals. Their biological cycle and mode of transmission involve an intermediate herbivorous host (locust, grasshopper, etc.) that picks up the pentastome's egg with its food. The larvae develop in the primary host, which is then caught and consumed by the final host. In chameleonids, the larvae migrate to the respiratory system and settle in the trachea, alveoli, etc. An infected chameleonid will cough up the newly laid eggs.

Pentastomes are whitish worms about 1 inch (2.5 cm) long. Prevention—by keeping wild-caught specimens separated from those that are captive-bred—is the best solution.

Endoparasites
Nemathelminthes (roundworms): The nematodes are smooth, round worms (ascarids, filarids). They are among the most common endoparasitic pests found in chameleonids. These migrating worms pass through the visceral organs, the digestive tract, or the lungs. Transmission occurs in two ways:

- Through the digestive tract by the ingesting of eggs or larvae, which then pass from the intestine to the bloodstream, creating microperforations (tiny holes). They eventually end their journey in the various organs of the chameleonid. The eggs of these worms are expectorated or excreted by the infested host.
- Through stinging insects such as mosquitoes (*Culex* sp.) or ticks of several genera. These blood-sucking creatures play the role of carrier, passing the microfilards into the bloodstream of the chameleonid. They mature and proceed to move about the host by perforating the tissues and visceral organs. They end their cycle by forming a cyst in a specific organ (e.g., the lungs for *Rhabdias gemellipara*, the stomach for *Physalopteroides chamaeleonis*, the intestines for *Hexametra angustaecoides*, or the subcutaneous tissues for *Foleyella furcata*). The activity of the parasites creates lesions, which in turn cause obstructions in the organs as well as hemorrhages, anemia, and the potential for secondary infections such as peritonitis or inflammation of the bronchial tubes.

Medical treatment is with Fenbendazole (Pancacen, Hoechst) 50 mg/kg administered orally.

Levimasole (Nemicide, ICI) 200 mg/kg administered orally is also effective. Repeat the procedure one month later.

Ivermectin (merck) was used in subcutaneous form in certain American king and corn snakes (*Lampropeltis* sp. and *Elaphe guttata*, respectively), at a dosage of 0.05 mg/kg orally once a week for two to six weeks. Medication was repeated at six-month intervals. The lethal dose for 100 percent of the snakes was 0.2 mg/kg. We tested Ivermectin (trade name Mectizan) in a number of Cameroonian chameleonids. At an oral dosage of 0.08 mg/kg no apparent toxification or organic disturbance was noted. Although Ivermectin prevents the development of macrofiliform eggs and larvae, it does not reduce the complications caused by cysts that the parasitic worms produce.

Platyhelminthes (tapeworms): Tapeworms (cestodes) and non-annulated flatworms (taenias) are found in smaller numbers than nematodes. The eggs of these worms are usually ingested when the mouths or tongues of the feeding chameleonids come into contact with infested soils. These worms take refuge in numerous organs.

Medical treatment is with Niclosamide (Bayer) 150 mg/kg orally, repeated in one month.

Dichlorophen (May & Baker) 200 mg/kg orally is also effective.

Trematodes (flukes): These flattened, non-annulated endoparasites are most commonly found in herbivorous lizards and tortoises. In chameleonids, the flukes occur in the bile ducts and in the intestine from the opening of the stomach to the cloaca.

The methods by which chameleonids develop trematode infestations are conjectural. The lizards may swallow larvae clustered on grasses in humid zones or consume snails and slugs that carry the parasites.

The pathological action of these parasites on chameleonids has not yet been studied. Since the chameleonid is the final host, the parasitic larvae mature and reproduce. The trematode eggs are then excreted by the chameleon.

Important note: All the medications for parasitic infestations mentioned in this discussion are available by prescription only. Consult your veterinarian.

Ectoparasites

Ectoparasites are external parasites, some of which are host-specific. They attack by piercing or cutting through the skin with specialized jaw parts. Among others, there are acarian mites, ticks, mosquitoes, leeches and flies. The acarian mites most plague the montane chameleons of the species *C. wiedersheimi, C. bitaeniatus,* and *C. quadricornis*, but they are also seen on the smaller *C. gastrotaenia* and *C. nasutus*. These chameleonids species often host numerous other parasites. If at all possible, avoid exposing farm-raised chameleonids to wild-collected potential carriers. Ticks may be easily removed by spreading a

Chamaeleo wiedersheimi.

mixture of one part oil and one part lindane (insecticide) on the tick.

Caution: This ointment is dangerous if applied to the skin of warm-blooded animals. Wear latex gloves when applying it; dispose of the gloves after use.

Clinical Procedures

How to Grasp and Hold a Chameleonid

Grasping a chameleonid by its nape, neck, spine, or tail will be interpreted by the animal as an aggressive gesture. It is usually best if you can encourage the chameleonid to hold you. By placing your hand under its neck and belly, then slowly and gently raising your hand upward, you can usually induce it to step onto your hand, where it will often cling tightly. If a fall seems imminent, gently enclose

Extreme care is essential when handling small species such as *Brookesia thieli.*

to grasp the gula (upper part of the throat) and pull downward carefully. The second method is less gentle than the first.

Oral Administration of Food and Medicine

If the specimen is able to eat, mix the medicine with the food. If the specimen refuses all nourishment, slip a catheter connected to a syringe down its throat to a point just behind to the animal's neck, and administer the contents.

How to Give Injections to Chameleonids

Subcutaneous injections can be made in the animal's flank. Gently pinch and lift up a bit of skin, then slip the needle quickly between the epidermis and dermis in this fold. Great care must be taken when giving intramuscular injections. Introduce the liquid into the muscle masses closest to the skin over the femur. Do not push the needle in too far.

Caution: Femoral shots are contraindicated when nephrotoxic drugs are being used.

Keeping the Chameleonid's Mouth Open

Cut a small piece of exposed film; fold it in half and cut a hole in the film that will allow you to observe the desired area of the mouth. Then insert the film, fold first, into the animal's mouth. To keep the film in place, you will need to hold both the film and the chameleonid's head.

the chameleon with the other hand, all the while allowing it to retain its grip. If absolutely necessary, immobilize it (as when medicating) by enfolding its body gently in one hand and folding the forelimbs backwards. Both hands may be needed to adequately restrain some large chameleon species.

How to Open a Chameleonid's Mouth

Gently pinch the animal's lips (behind the nostrils and in front of the eyes) and maintain pressure. The animal will soon open its mouth. Take care that you are not bitten in the process. With adults of some of the smaller chameleonid species (*C. nasutus, Brookesia* sp., *Rhampholeon* sp., etc.) and baby chameleonids, it may be necessary

Diagnostic Aids

Palpation

Examination by touch often allows us to locate the painful area and the reason for the animal's discomfort. By gently placing a finger on the sore area, one can sometimes actually hear the chameleon "groaning" (see page 25). Palpation often helps avoid diagnostic errors.

X-rays

An X-ray can be used to diagnose osteodystrophy, kidney stones, skeletal deformities, encystment, or visceral lesions. Films currently available to radiologists provide excellent definition to both bone and soft tissues.

Blood Test

To check for parasitic infestation, a drop of blood is taken. The veterinarian will disinfect the area, make a slight incision, and disinfect again.

Autopsy/Necropsy

An autopsy/necropsy can prove useful when the cause of a chameleonid's death is unknown. For the most accurate results, take the animal to a specialized laboratory (veterinary school or other) as soon after death as possible.

Summary: The veterinarian must take into account all possible causal factors and potential illnesses. The animal's background information (origin, feeding habits, and general behavior) is of great value in diagnosis.

Anesthesia

To ease the pain of most operations, suitable anesthetics must be used. Depending on the type and extent of the operation, either a general or a local anesthetic will be required. To preclude anesthetic-induced problems, the safest and most suitable type for the intended procedure must always be sought.

Halothane (Fluothane, I.C.I.) is the preferred anesthetic when general anesthesia is required. It is an inhalable gas that must be administered very carefully and in a special vaporizer.

A mixture of 3 percent pure oxygen per 15 ml of Halothane per m^3 will put the animal to sleep quickly. Once anesthesia is induced, the amount of Halothane should be decreased to 1 percent in the same oxygen mixture. This is sufficient to prolong sleep.[1]

Important notes:
- Anesthetics should be administered only by veterinarians.
- The use of chloroform, ether, barbiturates, and numerous other sedatives can prove dangerous or even deadly to chameleonids.

Euthanasia

Wrap the animal in a towel, then place it in the freezer.

Death will be painless.

---

[1]J. E. Cooper, "Manual of anaesthesia for small animal practice," pp. 109–122, C. M. Ash and R. M. Furber, eds. BSAVA, London.

Chapter 13

Understanding Chameleonids

A Few Words on Chameleonid Psychology

"This is anthropocentrism!" I can hear the indignant voices of some purist readers. Yet many people who have observed and kept these lizards for quite some time firmly believe that chameleons are probably the most sensitive members of the reptile kingdom.

Look into a chameleonid's eyes when it is watching you. You will see fear, inquisitiveness, happiness, or whatever other emotion the animal is feeling reflected in its dilating and retracting pupils. Body language should also be studied.

Chamaeleo minor (female).

Interpreting Chameleonids' Body Language

Mannerism	Meaning
Crawling in front of the glass of the terrarium	An expression of discomfort. The chameleonid is stressed or unhappy. Lighting is insufficient or temperature is becoming too warm.
Bobbing head	Claiming territory. Courtship behavior if vivid pattern is evident
Gaping mouth	Aggression
Gaping mouth with dark coloration an hissing	Extreme anger after being attacked or great fright
Gaping mouth with pale coloration	Overheated. Needs immediate cooling
Closing the eyes for abormally long periods, even under normal conditions	Illness
Closing the eyes and hiding from another chameleon	Sign of being frightened by/of a cagemate
Vivid coloration with/without dark spots	Contentment/excitement
Vivid coloration with dark spots, gaping, and tail lashing	Anger
Pale coloration, chin and jaw idly resting on branch, tail coiled	Sleep position. Sign of relaxation
Vivid coloration with bright but sunken eyes	Thirst. (Dehydration can be determined by gently pinching the belly skin. Under normal conditions the skin should be supple and the pinched area should not remain visible.)
Dark coloration with submissive behavior; sleep posture when lying in the palm of the hand	I want to be petted/I enjoy being petted.

Remember: Never pinch or grasp a chameleonid by the neck or back-bone. Chameleonids interpret this as a very threatening gesture.

Chapter 14

Some Interesting Chameleonid Species

I feel qualified to offer comments and recommendations on the many species of chameleonids with which I have had personal experience. Some are hardier than others; some are most certainly prettier than others. Among those with which I have worked are many species that are now bred with some degree of regularity in captivity.

I have attempted to rate the species according to the degree of ease with which they are kept cap-

tive. In the discussions that follow, I have used the following terms:

- "Beginners," meaning that I have found the species easy to breed and a good pet
- "Intermediate," indicating that this is a species with which you will probably do well after gaining some experience with chameleon husbandry
- "Advanced," designating the very few species that are very demanding in husbandry parameters

The floor of a high equatorial forest. The temperature is cool or moderate throughout the year; rainfall and humidity are high. The plants that thrive here can tolerate low light and are ideal for the average apartment.

Rhampholeon spectrum in a threatening posture.

that follows. To find the correct husbandry parameters for the species in the column on the left, refer in the text to the species with which it has been cross-referenced in the column on the right.

The chameleonids mentioned in the following accounts are all generally available, though some may not be easily obtainable at all times.

I have cross-referenced many species with similar habits in the list

Stump-tailed Chameleons

Because of their dull coloration and quiet demeanor, stump-tailed chameleons are often overlooked by terrarium keepers. However, recreating a forest terrarium to which this ombrophilous (rain-loving) tropophilous (climatic change-

For	Refer To
C. bifidus	*C. p. parsonii*
C. belalandaensis	*C. antimena*
C. boettgeri	*C. montium*
C. malthe	*C. b. brevicornis*
C. brevicornis hilleniusi	*C. campani*
C. cristatus	*Rhampholeon spectrum*
C. cucullatus	*C. globifer*
C. deremensis	*C. quadricornis*
C. dilepis	*C. g. gracilis/C. senegalensis*
C. eisentrauti	*C. quadricornis*
C. fuelleborni	*C. jacksonii xantholophus*
C. gastrotaenia	*C. globifer*
C. höhnelii	*C. jacksonii xantholophus*
C. labordi	*C. antimena*
C. nasutus	*C. montium*
C. owenii	*C. g. gracilis*
C. rhinoceratus	*C. verrucosus*
C. tigris	*C. g. gracilis*
C. werneri	*C. jacksonii xantholophus*
C. wiedersheimi	*C. quadricornis*

loving) species can adapt to is an ambitious and challenging undertaking.

Rhampholeon spectrum spectrum, Bucholz, 1874; one additional subspecies—*R. s. boulengeri*, Steindachner, 1911: advanced.

Distribution and habitat
Distribution: Widespread in equatorial central Africa to an elevation of 5,550 feet (1,650 m).
Climate preferences: Shady and rainy habitats in damp, slightly cool forests.
Forest strata: Undergrowth in equatorial or mountain forests, from ground level to about 7 feet (2 m) high in shrubbery.
Status in the wild: Common.

Breeding Data
Breeding potential: Good.
Number of eggs per clutch: 2 to 4.
Number of clutches per year: 2 or 3.

Brookesia stumpffi.

Hatching time: 4 to 6 weeks at 73°F (22.5°C).
Sexual maturity: 3 months.

Terrarium Care
Terrarium type: Forest.
Sociability: Good.
Food: Feeds readily on small insects, termites, flies, etc.
Comments: This species does well in captivity. Although less spectacular than the typical chameleon, it is pleasantly colored and reasonably active. Many people find creating a primary forest terrarium an irresistible challenge. The temperature must be kept between 72 and 77°F (22–25°C). Relative humidity should be maintained at between 85 and 100 percent.

Brookesia stumpffi, Boettger, 1894: advanced.

Distribution and habitat
Distribution: Northern Madagascar.
Climate preferences: Likes rather warm/hot weather. Very active during the rainy period.
Forest strata: From the ground to 3 feet (1 m) high, in bushes.
Status in the wild: Localized.

Breeding Data
Breeding potential: Good.
Number of eggs per clutch: 3 to 5 (8 according to P. de Vosjoli—personal communication).
Number of clutches per year: 1 to 2.
Hatching time: 4 to 6 weeks at 75°F (24°C).
Sexual maturity: 5 months.

Terrarium Care

Terrarium type: Forest edge/deciduous primary forest.
Sociability: Good.
Food: Small insects.
Comments: *Brookesia stumpffi* is a very beautiful stump-tailed chameleon. It is lively, husky, and as hardy as many other species, such as *B. perarmata*. It is found in dry volcanic and calcareous forests (Amber Mountain) where the trees of this forest lose their leaves in dry seasons (tropophilous or deciduous primary forest). Stump-tails of this species emerge only when the rains arrive and the relative humidity is high (85 percent and above). *B. stumpffi* prefers temperatures of 77 to 82°F (25–28°C). This species goes into hibernation or aestivation when the season becomes too cool or too dry. Mating occurs during the rainy seasons (October–November, March–April).

Brookesia superciliaris, Kühl, 1820: advanced.

Distribution and Habitat
Distribution: Eastern primary forest of Madagascar.
Climate preferences: Moderate temperatures in shady, rainy habitats.
Forest strata: This terrestrial species occurs at altitudes of up to 2,000 feet (600 m).
Status in the wild: Common and widespread.

Breeding Data
Breeding potential: Good.

Number of eggs per clutch: 2 to 4.
Number of clutches per year: 2 to 3.
Hatching time: 4 weeks at 74°F (23°C).
Sexual maturity: 4 to 5 months.

Terrarium Care
Terrarium type: Forest.
Sociability: Good.
Food: Small insects, termites, fruit flies.
Comments: Widely scattered in the primary forests of eastern Madagascar. It varies morphologically, depending on the region inhabited. *B. superciliaris* enjoys high humidity (85 to 100 percent) and a temperature of 72–77°F (22–25°C).

Brookesia superciliaris is difficult to detect among dead leaves.

Brookesia thieli, Brygoo and Domergue, 1968: advanced.

Distribution and Habitat
Distribution: Forests of eastern central Madagascar.
Climate preferences: Sciophilous and ombrophilous, this species likes cool temperatures and rather humid areas.
Forest strata: Ground and shrubs.
Status in the wild: Abundant and localized.

Breeding Data
Breeding potential: Good.
Number of eggs per clutch: 2.
Number of clutches per year: 2.
Hatching time: 4 to 8 weeks at 72°F (22.5°C).
Sexual maturity: 5 months.

Terrarium Care
Terrarium type: Cold forest.
Sociability: Good.

Food: Small insects and invertebrates.
Comments: *Brookesia thieli* is found at 2,500 to 3,500 feet (750–1,000 m) in primary forest. It lives much the same way as *B. superciliaris* and hibernates from June to September under dead leaf masses or underground.

Chameleons

A. *Bradypodion sp.* Dwarf chameleons
Dwarf chameleons have the reputation of being robust and prolific. A female can give birth to more than 40 babies per year. Adults measure between 5 and 8 inches (12–20 cm). The males are very territorial and compete to display the brightest colors, while the females remain dull.

Bradypodion pumilum (male).

These chameleons are no longer exported from South Africa, but specimens can be obtained in Europe or the United States from private breeders.

Very active a large part of the year, these chameleons hibernate from May or June to September. They also appreciate high relative humidity in their terrarium and a temperature that does not exceed 81°F (27°C).

Bradypodion pumilum, Gmelin, 1789: advanced.

Distribution and Habitat
Distribution: Western Cape Province, South Africa.
Climate preferences: This is a heliophilous species of moderate Mediterranean-type climates.
Forest strata: Coastal bushes.
Status in the wild: Abundant.

Breeding Data
Breeding potential: Good.
Number of babies per litter: 5 to 12.
Number of litters per year: 3.
Gestation time: 4 months.
Sexual maturity: 8 months.

Terrarium Care
Terrarium Type: Plateau.
Sociability: Aggressive.
Food: Small insects, snails, lizards.
Comments: This little chameleon measures from 5.2 to 7.6 inches (13–19 cm). The females are smaller than the males. The gular crest is well developed, and the dorsal crest consists of a series of conical scales that can extend up to two-thirds of the way down the tail. The biology of the species is fairly well known. The chameleon colonies are very active during the hot season (October to April), during which the females can produce up to 3 litters. Animals of this species hibernates by taking refuge in burrows, which they dig or sometimes find haphazardly.

Bradypodion damaranum, Boulenger, 1887: advanced.

Distribution and Habitat
Distribution: Rainy coastal forests of the Cape Province.
Climate preferences: Cool rain forests.
Forest strata: Forest canopy, giant ferns.
Status in the wild: Localized.

Breeding Data
Breeding potential: Good.
Number of babies per litter: 5 to 12.
Number of litters per year: 2.
Gestation time: 4 to 5 months.
Sexual maturity: 8 months.

Terrarium Care
Terrarium type: High mountain.
Sociability: Aggressive.
Food: Small insects, snails, lizards.
Comments: Measures from 4.8 inches to 6.8 inches (12–17 cm), the males being larger and having more color (green and brown) than the females. This species appreciates a cool environment and very high humidity (85–100 percent). In the morning these animals take refuge in the treetops to bask in the sun

Bradypodion damaranum (top, male; bottom, female).

and then come down to seek cooler air and humidity.

Bradypodion dracomontanum, Raw, 1976: advanced.

Distribution and Habitat
Distribution: Mount Drakensberg, South Africa.
Climate preferences: This ombrophilous species likes rather cool and damp climates.
Forest strata: Rain forest and very humid prairies.
Status in the wild: Localized.

Breeding Data
Breeding potential: Good.
Number of babies per litter: 8 to 14.
Number of litters per year: 2.
Gestation time: 4 months.
Sexual maturity: 8 months.

Terrarium Care
Terrarium type: High mountain.
Sociability: Aggressive toward others of its species.
Food: Small insects, snails, lizards.
Comments: Identical to *B. damaranum* in needs.

Bradypodion thamnobates, Raw, 1976: beginners.

Distribution and Habitat
Distribution: Natal midlands, South Africa.
Climate preferences: This sun-loving species can withstand cool/cold days.
Forest strata: Bushes.
Status in the wild: Localized (Restricted according to South African *Red Data Book*).

Breeding Data
Breeding potential: Good.
Number of babies per litter: 7 to 20.
Number of litters per year: 1 to 2.
Gestation time: 3 to 4 months.
Sexual maturity: 8 months.

Terrarium Care
Terrarium type: Plateau.
Sociability: Males are aggressive toward each other.
Food: Small insects, snails, lizards.
Comments: This beautiful dwarf chameleon is now being bred in some numbers in captivity.

Bradypodion thamnobates (male).

B. *Chamaeleo* sp. Chameleons

This is by far the most varied and most astonishing group in the chameleonid family. Large numbers of the African species are found in a wide region extending from Cameroon to Tanzania. Fully one-third of the known chameleon species are found in Madagascar. The sizes and shapes are astonishingly diverse; the smallest species, *C. nasutus*, measures 4 inches (10 cm) at most, while *C. p. parsonii* can reach 8 times that size.

Chameleo antimena, Grandidier, 1872: advanced.

Distribution and Habitat
Distribution: Southwestern Madagascar.

Climate preferences: This sexually dimorphic species likes hot and sunny weather.
Forest strata: Bushes/shrubs.
Status in the wild: Abundant.

Breeding Data
Breeding potential: Good.
Number of eggs per clutch: 8 to 23.
Number of clutches per year: 2 to 3.
Hatching time: 7 to 8 months at 77°F (25°C).
Sexual maturity: 6 months.

Terrarium Care
Terrarium type: Sudano-Guinean/forest edge (in the wild, riparian stretches of forest).
Sociability: Aggressive.

Chamaeleo antimena (male).

Food: Insects, small animals.

Comments: *C. antimena* is happy as long as light, heat, and food are abundant. Sexually receptive females show particularly beautiful patterns that keep the males very interested.

Chamaeleo b. brevicornis, Günther, 1879: beginners

Distribution and Habitat

Distribution: Eastern central Madagascar.

Climate preferences: Rainy, damp forests.

Forest strata: Bushes and trees.

Status in the wild: Abundant.

Breeding Data

Breeding potential: Good.

Number of eggs per clutch: 5 to 16.

Number of clutches per year: 2.

Hatching time: 5 months at 72°F (22.5°C).

Sexual maturity: 8 months.

Terrarium Care

Terrarium type: Plateau.

Sociability: Average.

Food: Same as other chameleons.

Comments: *C. brevicornis* is easy

to keep happy in a suitable terrarium. Often available as young farm-raised specimens, they will reach adulthood in 8 months. A short resting period (one month) is necessary. This species can withstand cool nights and days 65°F (18°C).

Chameleo c. calyptratus, Dumeril, 1851: beginners.

Distribution and Habitat
Distribution: High plateau and grasslands of Yemen.
Climate preferences: Sun-loving.

Forest strata: Bushes, shrubs, cultivated zones; found on eucalyptus.
Status in the wild: Abundant.

Breeding Data
Breeding potential: Good.
Number of eggs per clutch: 30 to 70.
Number of clutches per year: 3.
Hatching time: 6 to 8 months (168–220 days) at 80°F (27°C).
Sexual maturity: 6 months.

Terrarium Care
Terrarium type: Sudanese/Sudano-Guinean.

Sociability: Males are extremely aggressive toward each other but coexist well with one or more females.

Food: Insects, small animals, leaves, blossoms.

Comments: *C. calyptratus* can be found in mountainous regions of northern Yemen at altitudes of 1,700 to 9,500 feet (510–2,850 m). On these plateaus the climate is tropical to subtropical and the vegetation exuberant. *C. calyptratus* lives in the forested stretches and is also present in certain valleys of southern Yemen, in which the habitat is very different from that of the plateaus. The valleys have a desert-type climate with dry winters and occasional periods of extreme cold.

This hardy, beautiful chameleon species is easy to care for. Males display beautiful sky-blue, green, yellow, and black liveries. It is bred in large numbers in many countries.

Additional comments about *C. calyptratus*: In the wild, during the dry season, this species eats the leaves of plants to find the water it cannot get from rain. The sexes of this species are easily differentiated. Males of all ages, hatchlings to adults, bear prominent tarsal spurs.

Chamaeleo campani, Grandidier, 1872: advanced.

Distribution and Habitat
Distribution: Plateau of eastern central Madagascar.

Chamaeleo calyptratus (male).

Climate preferences: Very humid and cool temperatures (an ombrophilous species).

Forest strata: Grass.

Status in the wild: Localized.

Breeding Data
Breeding potential: Difficult.

Number of eggs per clutch: 8 to 12.

Number of clutches per year: 2 to 3.

Hatching time: 9 months at 68°F (20°C).

Sexual maturity: 3 months.

Terrarium Care
Terrarium type: Plateau prairie.

Sociability: Good.

Food: Grasshoppers.

Comments: This small chameleon is found on the prairies of high

Chamaeleo
campani
(male).

plateaus, near the edge of primary forests. The air in these regions is almost always saturated with humidity. The relative humidity is often 100 percent.

More about *C. campani:* This species may be related to the *C.*

Chamaeleo
campani
(female).

verrucosus group. In winter, snow can be found on the prairies where *C. campani* lives.

Too high a temperature during the incubation of this species results in birth defects. The hatchlings of this dimorphically patterned species bear the same markings as the adults; thus they are easily sexed at birth.

Chamaeleo chamaeleon, Linnaeus, 1758: beginners.

Distribution and Habitat
Distribution: North Africa, parts of southern Europe.
Climate preferences: A heliophilous species, the common chameleon enjoys high temperatures.
Forest strata: Shrubs, bushes, trees.
Status in the wild: Abundant.

Breeding Data
Breeding potential: Good.
Number of eggs per clutch: 15 to 50.
Number of clutches per year: 1 or 2.
Hatching time: 8 to 9 months at 77°F (25°C).
Sexual maturity: 7 months.

Terrarium Care
Terrarium type: Sudanese.
Sociability: Aggressive.
Food: Small animals, insects, snails.
Comments: This is often an easy species for novices. Commonly found in oases and on the edge of all areas with a supply of water, it takes refuge in groves and thickets when the weather is too hot. This chameleon is found at altitudes so high that people claim to have

found it under a blanket of snow. It is certainly one of the less demanding species in captivity.

Chamaeleo f. fischeri, Reichebow, 1887: 5 subspecies: *C. fischeri excubitor, C. f. multituberculatus, C. f. tavetanus, C. f. uluguruensis, C. f. uthmolleri:* advanced.

Distribution and Habitat
Distribution: Lush plateaus of East Africa, in Kenya and Tanzania.
Climate preferences: Likes to sun, but is most common in damp areas.
Forest strata: Shrubs, bushes, prairies.
Status in the wild: Common.

Breeding Data
Breeding potential: Good.
Number of eggs per clutch: 15 to 32.
Number of clutches per year: 2 or 3.
Hatching time: 5 months at 73.5°F (23°C).
Sexual maturity: 6 months.

Terrarium Care
Terrarium type: Plateau prairie.
Sociability: Aggressive toward others of its species.
Food: Flies, locusts, small insects, snails, and lizards.
Comments: This impressive species needs a large and sunny terrarium. *C. f. tavetanus,* which originated in Kenya, has been bred successfully in Germany. The eggs have to be kept for 4 to 5 months at 71°F (21.5°C).

Chamaeleo fischeri fischeri (male).

Chamaeleo globifer, Günther, 1879: intermediate and advanced.

Distribution and Habitat
Distribution: Eastern forests of Madagascar.
Climate preferences: Cool, humid areas.
Forest strata: Trees.
Status in the wild: Localized.

Breeding Data
Breeding potential: Average to poor.
Number of eggs per clutch: 30 to 50.
Number of clutches per year: 1.
Hatching time: 8 months at 70°F (21°C).
Sexual maturity: 8 months.

Chamaeleo fischeri tavetanus (male).

Terrarium Care

Terrarium type: Plateau.
Sociability: Aggressive.
Food: Insects.
Comments: To be kept in the same way as *C. lateralis,* but this species prefers a more humid atmosphere.

Chamaeleo gracilis, Hallowell, 1842: beginners.

Distribution and Habitat

Distribution: Central Africa.
Climate preferences: Typical equatorial species, fond of heat and humidity.
Forest strata: Trees and shrubs.
Status in the wild: Abundant.

Breeding Data

Breeding potential: Reasonable.

Number of eggs per clutch: 20 to 40.
Number of clutches per year: 1 or 2.
Hatching time: 6 months at 74°F (23.5°C).
Sexual maturity: 4 to 5 months.

Terrarium Care

Terrarium type: Forest.
Sociability: Quite aggressive.
Food: Every moving thing that can be caught by the tongue and carried into the mouth.
Comments: Widely scattered throughout central Africa, west to east. Aged females of this species sometimes measure up to 15 inches (38 cm) in total length. It is a typically equatorial species, enjoying humidity and heat.

Chamaeleo globifer juvenile.

106

Chamaeleo j. jacksonii, Boulenger, 1896: beginners.

Distribution and Habitat
Distribution: Mountains of Kenya and Tanzania.
Climate preferences: Foggy damp and cool places.
Forest strata: Shrubs and sometimes trees.
Status in the wild: Widespread.

Breeding Data
Breeding potential: Good.
Number of babies per litter: 8 to 35.
Number of litters per year: 2.
Gestation time: 5 to 6 months.
Sexual maturity: 5 to 6 months.

Terrarium Care
Terrarium type: High mountain.
Sociability: Males are aggressive.
Food: Caterpillars, snails, spiders, flies.
Comments: *C. j. xantholophus* is very popular with the general public. This species likes high humidity and cool temperatures.

C. jacksonii merumontanus, a subspecies, is smaller and sometimes brighter in color.

Species capable of living in the same conditions: *C. höhnelii, C. fülleborni, C. rudis, C. eliotti.*
Additional comments: Female *C. jacksonii xantholophus* give bith twice a year. A large litter is generally dropped in June, another, smaller, one by December. High humidity and suitable temperature are the signals for the females to drop their babies. If the weather is not favorable, they can hold them for several weeks. A female kept outside in adverse winter weather may retain her babies and eventually die. The females of this subspecies show no nasal horns; the female of *C. j. jacksonii* bears three rudimentary horns as a baby, but only a single nasal appendage when adult.

Chamaeleo johnstoni, Boulenger, 1901: beginners to advanced.

Distribution and Habitat
Distribution: This species can be found at altitudes of 3,000 to 8,500 feet (900–2,500 m) in the mountains of Burundi, Rwanda, and Zaire.

Climate preferences: Rainy regions of variable temperature.
Forest strata: Trees.
Status in the wild: Abundant.

Breeding Data
Breeding potential: Good.
Number of eggs per clutch: 8 to 23.
Number of clutches per year: 3.
Hatching time: 4 months at 72°F (22.5°C) (±100 days)
Sexual maturity: 5 months.

Terrarium Care
Terrarium type: High mountain.
Sociability: Aggressive.
Food: Flies, grasshoppers, spiders, snails.
Comments: As long as high humidity is maintained, this is an easy species for novices. It does extremely well in high-mountain terrariums. The species has been successfully bred several times.

Chamaeleo lateralis, Gray, 1851; second subspecies, C. lateralis major, now known: beginners.

Distribution and Habitat
Distribution: Widespread on the plateau of Madagascar.
Climate preferences: A sun-loving species.
Forest strata: Bushes.
Status in the wild: Widespread and common.

Breeding Data
Breeding potential: Good.
Number of eggs per clutch: 8 to 23.
Number of clutches per year: 3.
Hatching time: 5 months at 74°F

(23.5°C) longer if incubation temperature is lower.
Sexual maturity: 3 months.

Terrarium Care

Terrarium type: Plateau.
Sociability: Fairly aggressive.
Food: Insects, small animals.
Comments: This species is found over a great part of Madagascar, at altitudes between 2,000 and 4,000 feet (600–1,200 m). It occurs in forests, on prairies, and even in cities. It lives on bushes or in trees. In drier areas, it shows a preference for the most humid places, such as the seaside or the banks of rivers.

It is a nice animal to keep in captivity. Its robustness, activity, lively character, and "flashy" colors make it a good choice for beginners. This species likes the sun and moderate temperatures, is territorial, and hibernates from June to September.

Chamaeleo lateralis major is the subspecies found on the southwest Madagascan coast. It differs from *C. lateralis* in its size, which can reach 14 inches.

Chamaeleo lateralis (female).

Additional comments about *C. lateralis:* In the wild, *C. lateralis* has a short life span—about a year and a half. In terrariums, farm-raised specimens can live more than 3 years.

Chamaeleo melleri, Gray, 1864: beginners to advanced.

Distribution and Habitat

Distribution: Savannas of southern Kenya, southern Malawi, and Tanzania.
Climate preferences: Hot places.

Chamaeleo melleri (male).

Forest strata: Trees.
Status in the wild: Dispersed.

Breeding Data
Breeding potential: Unknown. Only a few have been bred in captivity.
Number of eggs per clutch: 15 to 45.
Number of clutches per year: 1.
Hatching time: 5 months at 73.5°F (23°C).
Sexual maturity: Unknown.

Terrarium Care
Terrarium type: Forest edge and forest.
Sociability: Average.
Food: Insects and small animals.
Comments: Contrary to what many people think, this species likes hot, rather humid climates. It is often found in the big trees of the Tanzanian savannas in small groups of up to 5.

Courtship and threatening behaviors can be very impressive. The males show their most brilliant colors, from blue to light yellow.

When it gets too hot, the chameleons take refuge in the foilage and display very light colors to avoid overheating.

Chamaeleo minor, Günther, 1879: beginners.

Distribution and Habitat
Distribution: Southern central plateau of Madagascar.
Climate preferences: Variable. Generally heliophilous.
Forest strata: Bushes, rarely trees.
Status in the wild: Localized.

Breeding Data
Breeding potential: Good.
Number of eggs per clutch: 11 to 16.
Number of clutches per year: 3.

Chamaeleo minor (male).

Hatching time: 9 months at 67°F (19.5°C).
Sexual maturity: 5 months.

Terrarium Care
Terrarium type: Plateau prairie and forest edge.
Sociability: Good.
Food: Insects.
Comments: Uncontestably a choice species for both amateurs and connoisseurs. This hardy, resistant species lives on the plateau plains in eastern central Madagascar. The females exibit an extraordinary array of colors, while the males, which on average are twice as large, are more quietly colored: brown, clear blue, and a sort of orange. The young are green at birth and display rapid growth. The young males' horns appear in the first two weeks of their existence; sexes are easily determined.

Chamaeleo m. montium, Buchholz, 1874; besides the nominate form, three subspecies: *C. montium feae, C. m. pfefferi, C. m. grafi:* advanced.

Distribution and Habitat
Distribution: Adamaua Chain (Cameroon mountain chain).
Climate preferences: Highest possible humidity, cool temperatures.
Forest strata: Shrubs, pine trees.
Status in the wild: Abundant.

Breeding Data
Breeding potential: Good.
Number of eggs per clutch: 8 to 15.

Number of clutches per year: 3 or 4.
Hatching time: 5 to 6 months incubated at 72.5°F (22.5°C).
Sexual maturity: 4 months.

Chamaeleo montium (female).

Terrarium Care
Terrarium type: High mountain.
Sociability: Fairly aggressive species.
Food: Flies, bugs.
Comments: These mountain chameleons are robust animals and not demanding as long as their humidity needs are fulfilled. In fact, near 100 percent humidity is to their liking. Chameleons of this species cannot tolerate heat or dryness. They must have a very cool and humid terrarium where their cool-toned colors (blue, green, lemon-yellow) will be very vivid. The climatic variations are identical to those for *C. quadricornis.*

Chamaeleo pardalis, Cuvier, 1829: beginners.

Distribution and Habitat
Distribution: Northern coast of Madagascar.

Chamaeleo pardalis (female).

Chamaeleo pardalis (male).

Climate preferences: Hot and humid climates.
Forest strata: Shrubs and trees.
Status in the wild: Abundant.

Breeding Data
Breeding potential: Good.
Number of eggs per clutch: 15 to 30.
Number of clutches per year: 2, sometimes 3.
Hatching time: 5 months at 76°F (24.5°C).
Sexual maturity: 5 months.

Terrarium Care
Terrarium type: Forest edge.
Sociability: Rather aggressive.
Food: Insects, frogs, small animals.
Comments: *Chamaeleo pardalis* is a very popular species for terrariophiles, because quite often its ecological needs correspond to the perceived need for heat and humidity. Further, it is easily tamed and displays remarkably variable and very beautiful shades of color. Specimens from northern Madagascar are especially colorful. Sexual activity is intense most of the year. This species is easily bred in captivity.

This chameleon does not require hibernation and must be kept at temperatures between 77–81°F (25–27°C) and a humidity level around 90 to 100 percent during the daytime. Cooler and a bit drier conditions can be maintained from June to September, but the temperature should never drop below 72°F (22.5°C).

Chamaeleo pardalis is very eclectic as far as meals are concerned. It will eat, besides the usual insect fare, small lizards, snails, and some small vertebrates.

The coloration of the babies indicates whether the baby is male or female. Females have a pink and dark brown pattern; males usually have more than two colors: the Nosy Bé morph has white, brown, yellow, and blue spots on the cheeks.

Chamaeleo parsonii, Cuvier, 1824; second subspecies, *C. parsonii cristifer*, has demanding habitat parameters: intermediate.

Distribution and Habitat
Distribution: Central eastern forests of Madagascar.
Climate preferences: Humid and cool places.
Forest strata: Canopy of trees.
Status in the wild: Localized.

Breeding Data
Breeding potential: Difficult.
Number of eggs per clutch: 40 to 60.
Number of clutches per year: 1.
Hatching time: Up to 21 months at 65°F (18°C).
Sexual maturity: 18 months.

Terrarium Care
Terrarium type: Plateau forest.
Sociability: Average to poor.
Food: Insects, lizards, sometimes birds.
Comments: This is arguably the largest chameleon species. Some males attain a length of more than

32 inches (81 cm). Found in rain forests along much of the east coast of Madagascar, it is a shy chameleon of rather quiet demeanor. Large specimens are often several years old.

The subspecies *C. parsonii cristifer,* localized in Périnet, is beautifully colored in a remarkable navy blue hue. *C. p. parsonii* likes cool temperatures and high relative humidity (90 to 100 percent) and is found in treetops. Its diet consists of invertebrates and small animals (including birds).

C. p. parsonii and the related species *C. balteatus* and *C. bifidus* mate after a period of rest brought on by a drop in temperature during the cold season (May to September). The females usually lay one clutch of eggs per year at the beginning of the cold season (May

to June). In captivity, reproduction occurs only after a period of rest.

Chamaeleo p. parsonii can be an interesting subject for a cold-forest type of terrarium. Maintain maximum humidity and avoid too much heat. From June to September, the animal's activity may slow down. The relative humidity of the air can be brought down to 75 to 80 percent and the light filtered so that the temperature drops to 62 to 72°F (17–22.5°C), but food must also be supplied.

The other members of the *C. parsonii* group are *C. balteatus, C. bifidus, C. furcifer, C. gastrotaenia, C. globifer, C. minor, C. oshaugnessyi,* and *C. willsii.*

More comments about *C. p. parsonii:* To successfully breed *C. p. parsonii,* you must be patient and follow these instructions:

- Keep 1 male for 2 or 3 females in a large enclosure where they can freely move around. They need large branches and, if possible, trees to climb.
- Have all the adults rest for at least 2 months in a cool, dark room.
- When the time has come for them to mate, put the males in the cage, then introduce the females and wait for them to mate.

Chamaeleo quadricornis, Tornier, 1899; second subspecies, _Chamaeleo quadricornis gracilior_ (see W. Böhme and J. J. Klaver, _Amphibia-Reptilia,_ 1981): beginners.

Distribution and Habitat
Distribution: Mount Manengouba, Cameroon.

Climate preferences: Moderate temperatures, rather high air humidity.
Forest strata: Shrubs.
Status in the wild: Localized but abundant.

Breeding Data
Breeding potential: Good.
Number of eggs per clutch: 8 to 15.
Number of clutches per year: 2 or 3.
Hatching time: 5 months at 72.5°F (22.5°C).
Sexual maturity: 6 months.

Terrarium Care
Terrarium type: High mountain.
Sociability: Average.
Food: Insects, flies, locusts.
Comments: The four-horn chameleon is found at 6,000 feet (1,800 m) in a region of semi-grassy savanna with extremely wet semi-forested areas.

Chamaeleo quadricornis (female).

All year the sunlight is filtered through the numerous clouds that cover the mountain chain of western Cameroon. The temperature ranges between 60 and 86°F (16–30°C) depending on the time of year.

A cool, dry season (62 percent relative humidity) begins by December or January, when the dry winds from northern Africa arrive. These winds are called the "Armattan," and persist for 7 to 30 days. The cool, "dry" season ends with the onset of the rainy season; all year, rain falls in abundance and the humidity of both the air and the earth remains near 100 percent.

All year *C. quadricornis* lives in a habitat with only slight climatic changes between the cool seasons (minimum 60° [16°C]) and the hot seasons (maximum 80.6°F [27°C]).

Female *Chamaeleo quadricornis* lay eggs 2 or 3 times a year: December/January, March/April, July/August. The maximum number of eggs is about 15. Laying sometimes occurs two months after mating. The geographic range of this chameleon (which is also found in the Tchabal Mbabo region) seems very small in relation to the density of the apparent population.

Male *C. quadricornis,* like all other chameleons of this mountain chain, are adorned with a dorsal crest, which extends in a fan onto the tail. Up to three (usually two) pairs of rather small annulated horns occur on the end of the snout.

This chameleon is a good terrarium subject. Robust and visually impressive, it often displays pastel shades that can be quite elegant. As with *C. wiedersheimi* or *C. montium sp.,* the crests may serve a purely ornamental function, intended to impress sexual rivals. The sex of the babies is determined by looking at the general livery, which is very similar in babies and adults.

Reproduction in the terrarium is achieved without difficulty.

Chamaeleo senegalensis, Daudin, 1802: beginners to advanced.

Distribution and Habitat
Distribution: Widely distributed in Africa.
Climate preferences: Warm and humid areas.
Forest strata: West African forest galleries along rivers, also savannas.
Status in the wild: Common.

Breeding Data
Breeding potential: Good.
Number of eggs per clutch: 25 to 60.
Number of clutches per year: 2.
Hatching time: 5 to 6 months at 76°F (24.5°C).
Sexual maturity: 5 months.

Terrarium Care
Terrarium type: Sudanese, forest edge.
Sociability: Aggressive.
Food: Insects, lizards, spiders.
Comments: *Chamaeleo senegalensis* was for years one of the most popular species in the pet trade

because it is very hardy, used to the rigorous weather of West Africa. Imported specimens are often weakened by internal parasites. It is a very prolific species, laying eggs twice a year. Eggs, generally laid in April or May at the end of the rainy season, hatch at the beginning of the next rainy season (August). Many of these babies will be consumed by other animals such as snakes, birds, and even other chameleons. This species likes damp and warm climates. It is usually found in the forest edge, where it finds shelter and food. Owing to almost inevitable parasite problems, I do not recommend specimens from the wild.

Chamaeleo verrucosus, Cuvier, 1829; second subspecies, *C. verrucosus semicristatus,* Boettger, 1894: advanced.

Distribution and Habitat
Distribution: Southern coastal Madagascar.
Climate preferences: Hot habitats with variable humidity.
Forest strata: Shrubs and trees.
Status in the wild: Widely scattered.

Breeding Data
Breeding potential: Good.
Number of eggs per clutch: 30 to 58.
Number of clutches per year: 1, rarely 2.

Chamaeleo verrucosus (female).

Chamaeleo willsii (male).

Chamaeleo willsii (female).

Hatching time: 7 months at 80°F (26.5°C).
Sexual maturity: 6 months.

Terrarium Care
Terrarium type: Sudano-Guinean.
Sociability: Tolerant to aggressive.
Food: Insects, lizards, small rodents, birds.
Comments: *C. verrucosus* is an inveterate basker. It lives in rather arid regions, but rarely far from the sea or other water.

C. oustaleti can live in the same conditions in southern Madagascar, where the rainy seasons last from December to February. From June to August the chameleons go underground to escape the cool, dry weather and survive when food is scarce. During this period of inactivity, air humidity can drop to 30 percent.

These two species reproduce in captivity without difficulty.

Chamaeleo willsii willsii, Günther, 1890; second subspecies, *C. willsii petteri,* E.-R. Brygoo, Ch. Domergue, 1966: advanced.

Distribution and Habitat
Distribution: Eastern central and southeastern Madagascar.
Climate preferences: Cool and humid.
Forest strata: Shrubs.
Status in the wild: Localized.

Breeding Data
Breeding potential: Good.

Number of eggs per clutch: 8 to 15.
Number of clutches per year: 1 or 2.
Hatching time: 5 months at 74°F (23.5°C).
Sexual maturity: 4 months.

Terrarium Care
Terrarium type: Plateau forest.
Sociability: Moderate.
Food: Insects (locusts).
Comments: *Chamaeleo w. willsii* is incontestably a charming little chameleon. Active, prettily colored, and moderately sociable, it is an excellent choice for a "cool" and humid terrarium. It lives on the great forest plateau of eastern Madagascar at altitudes between 3,000 and 3,300 feet (900–1,000 m). It is most often found in bushes.

C. willsii petteri lives in northern Madagascar, in the forests of Joffreville and in the massif of Ankarana. It is largely a canopy form.

C. w. willsii, a lively animal, is more sociable than *C. willsii petteri.* It seldom bites and is less aggressive than many other chameleon species.

During cool weather these chameleons "hibernate" several days per week (June to September). They take refuge in dead forest leaves or in a burrow. They occasionally come out of their retreats to eat and drink when it warms up.

Conclusion

Science strives to answer humanity's anguished "Whys?" But before we can understand a part of our universe, we must find ourselves awed by the spectacle. Wonder is the first step to knowledge; love is the first step to happiness.

Recreating a habitat in a terrarium, simple as it may be, is an exciting and gratifying enterprise. Maintaining such a microcosm can help us study a small part of our world and its special logic.

True animal lovers respect, admire, and try to understand the creatures that they raise. This is why I hope that, here and there, dedicated efforts will be made to nurture fauna in captivity so they can thrive and be shared. If these efforts are successful, the majority of chameleons acquired as pets soon will be farm raised. This will allow hobbyists to obtain healthy animals, accustomed to human contact, whose age and genetic background are known.

At Marozevo we are developing the chameleons of the future! These animals will have livelier natures and brighter colors. Eventually, hybridization will provide us with completely new varieties; while controlled breeding will serve equally to protect endangered species and lead to a better understanding of chameleon biology.

I rejoice at the progress that such farming programs bring to nature and to humankind; and I wish you, dear reader, much success with your own chameleons.

Brookesia peramata; an enclosure at Marozevo (inset).

Useful Literature and Addresses

Organizations and Publications

American Federation of
  Herpetoculturists (A.F.H.)
P.O. Box 300067
Escondido, California 92030-0067
(619) 747-4948
  The A.F.H. is a nonprofit organization that seeks to protect the rights of private collectors and breeders of reptiles and amphibians in the U.S.A. Membership entitles you to receive *The Vivarium,* an excellent magazine that is highly regarded by professionals and private breeders.

Captive Breeding Magazine
P.O. Box 87100
Canton, Michigan 48187
(313) 454-0700
  Another very good magazine with emphasis on captive breeding.

Chameleon Information Network
  c/o Ardi Abate
13419 Appalachian Way
San Diego, California 92129
(619) 484-2669

This American-European-South African working group on chameleons publishes a newsletter four times a year. Over 200 correspondents worldwide, include scientists, breeders, private collectors, and naturalists. Seeks to promote the knowledge of chameleons, their care, and their breeding in controlled environments.

Secretariaat Doelgroep Kameleons
Sanma Van Duin
Dotterbloemstraat 16
3286 VM Klaanswaal
The Netherlands
(International)-31 1864-3984
  A very large and active working group of private breeders and zoo curators. They gather once or twice a year in Holland for a special international meeting where captive-bred chameleons can be bought and sold.

Reptiles
P.O. Box 6050
Mission Viejo, California 92690
(815) 734-60863
  A specialized magazine on reptiles, which complements *The Vivarium.*

Breeders and Importers

If you are unable to obtain a particular species locally, you might try the following mail-order sources.

Agama International Inc.
Rd #2
(*Bradypodion thamnobates*)
Bert Langerwerf
Box 285
Monterallo, Alabama 35115

Fluker Farms
(*Chamaeleo calyptratus* and food)
Baton Rouge, Louisiana 70821
(800) 735-8537 X50

The Marozevo Breeding Farm
BP6218, Fenomanana
Antananarivo 101, Madagascar
No, I cannot send you chameleons, but if you plan to visit Madagascar, you are welcome to drop in at the farm for a short stop. If you are a chameleon lover, the stop may last for several days! More than 35 species of chameleons are bred here in huge cages. In addition to many other animals (birds, insects, frogs, mammals) you are bound to meet some of the scientists and students who participate in local projects for endangered species.

Reptile Specialties
John Uhern
P.O. Box 31, 7473 Foothill Boulevard
Tujunga, California 91042
(818) 352-1796

SandFire Dragon Ranch
(*Chamaeleo calyptratus*)
Robert Mailloux
P.O. Box 3152
Vista, California 92085

Food and Supplies

Specialty items that you cannot obtain locally may be ordered from the following mail-order suppliers.

Expobait
(Butterworms)
8030 Deerfield St.
San Diego, California 92120
(619) 582-8862

Ghann's Cricket Farm Inc.
P.O. Box 211840-R
Augusta, Georgia 30917-1840
(800) 476-2248

Grubco
Box 15001
Hamilton, Ohio 45015
(800) 222-3563

Nekton USA Inc.
14405 60th Street North
Clearwater, Florida 34620
(813) 530-3500

Rainbow Mealworms
126 E. Spruce Street
P.O. Box 4907
Compton, California 90224
1 (800) 777-9676

Rep-Cal Research Labs
(Calcium carbonate from oyster
  shells)
P.O. Box 727
Los Gatos, California 95031
(408) 356-4289

Reptile Specialties
(Dietary supplements for
  chameleons, live food)
(See page 123.)

Zeigler Brothers Inc. Reptile Food
P.O. Box 21126
Detroit, Michigan 48221
(313) 345-5388

*Bradypodion
thamnobates*

Index

Numerals in **bold face type** indicate color photographs.